THE 10-WEEK
FLEXIBLE INVESTMENT PLAN

A BEGINNER'S GUIDE TO STOCK MARKET SUCCESS

ALEXANDER DAVIDSON

KOGAN
PAGE

First published in 2003 by Kogan Page Limited

Kogan Page Limited
120 Pentonville Road
London N1 9JN
United Kingdom

www.kogan-page.co.uk

British Library Cataloguing in Publication Data

A CIP record for this book is available from the British Library.

ISBN 0 7494 3885 1

Typeset by JS Typesetting Ltd, Wellingborough, Northants
Printed and bound in Great Britain by Biddles Ltd, Guildford and King's Lynn
www.biddles.co.uk

For Aigulia,
who has brought warmth and brightness into my life.
This book is for you darling, with all my love.

Contents

Foreword

Once upon a time, not so very long ago, it was all so very easy. Being a private investor seemed a licence to print money. All you had to do was read the latest tip in the *Daily Blah* or earwig a conversation between a couple of Arthur Daileys in the pub, buy the shares and sit smugly while the price shot skywards. It didn't really matter what the company did – usually it was something mysterious involving the Internet or mobile phones – we were enjoying a raging bull market and millions of new investors watched their worldly wealth multiply.

Of course, it couldn't last and it didn't. With a speed that left unwary investors breathless and bereft, the bear market arrived and share values plummeted. Those who had assumed that the market would climb forever had not taken the precaution of harvesting profits and so discovered that their journey to millionaire status was all an illusion. Many of them retired, hurt and with a sense of failure, from the shares game.

But there are those who work to the maxim that mistakes are only disasters if you don't learn from them. They recognized the bear market for what it was, simply a change in the investing climate that, properly managed, presented as many opportunities as it stifled. The movement from bulls to bears was inevitable, and it is just as certain that the good times will return. Astute investors will be able to make money from the stock market no matter what the indices are doing and indeed they can harness the price movements to enhance their performance. There is a proviso though, like any job or hobby you will never be really good at it unless you are aware of what is going on. You accept the pitfalls and know how to avoid them, you recognize the opportunities and have learned how to exploit them.

It is for those people, the would-be winners who want to play the shares game and are prepared to understand exactly what they are doing, that Alexander Davidson has written his book. And in doing so he has produced a publication that should have a place on the bookshelf of every private investor because he has assumed nothing and avoided the annoying jargon of the stockmarket.

I have read enough investment books to know that all but a few fall into two categories: utterly boring or too complicated. The only ones that have a formula for success are those that are:

- understandable;
- fun to read;
- interesting;
- informative;
- testing for the brain.

Mr Davidson has satisfied all the criteria. In these pages he has covered almost every aspect of investing and in doing so he has done a considerable service for the private investor. Read it carefully and, in particular, have a go at the quizzes that end each chapter. No matter what your level of investment knowledge you will have fun finding out what you didn't know.

The 10-Week Flexible Investment Plan is both a page-turner and a book of reference. You should profit from reading it.

Terry Bond
Development Director, Proshare

Acknowledgements

Thanks to Jon Finch, my editor, Martha Fumagalli who runs publicity, Heather Langridge and others at Kogan Page for helping so much to develop my writing career.

My gratitude to colleagues on the IFR equities desk, and to my many friends, contacts and colleagues in the City. Without you, I would not have been able to write this book.

Thanks to Connie King for her excellent Web design.

My thanks also to Natasha Roschina in St Petersburg for contributing the charts. Good luck for the future.

Wealth warning

The investment methods described in this book have worked exceptionally well for some investors in the past in both good and bad market conditions, but may not suit everybody all of the time. This book is for educational purposes only, and in no way offers special investment advice. Also, the author has made every effort to ensure the book is up to date, but things change. Ultimately, any investments that you make are at your own risk.

About the author

Alexander Davidson is one of the country's leading financial journalists and a regular guest contributor to national newspapers. In his previous career he worked as a share dealer, specializing in small, high-growth companies. Disillusioned with the biased advice that some City firms were offering, he quit his job and set up as an independent writer and consultant. Next came the publication of his best-selling exposé book *The City Share Pushers*. Serial rights were bought by News International for a record sum and Channel 4's *Dispatches* turned the book into an acclaimed documentary. The book formed the basis of a motion passed in the House of Commons and reputedly changed the way the City operates.

Since then, Alexander has written a number of other books, including the best-sellers *How to Win in a Volatile Stock Market* and *Everyone's Guide to Online Stock Market Investing*, both published by Kogan Page. Recently, he worked on the trading floor of a top investment bank. He holds the Securities Institute Diploma and an accounting qualification, and is a qualified, experienced instructor as well as an avid private investor. In the *Book of Investing Rules* published by Global-Investor.com, the author is recognized as one of the elite of investing, among the best in the world.

Introduction

To start investing in stocks and shares is exciting but difficult as well. You will meet a small army of so-called experts who have answers to any questions that you may put them. They all want your money.

If you are to survive as an investor, you will need to make your own decisions. Above all, you need to be flexible. Without this, you can lose serious money very quickly.

I am pleased to say that many investors have acknowledged this. When I set up my Web site, Flexible Investment Strategies (www.flex-invest.co.uk), to help investors, I was staggered by the high level of hits I received. The response convinced me of the urgent need for a book that covers the basics of flexible stock market investing.

I know that you are busy, but want to use your time for investing to best effect. It is to help you in this endeavour that I have prepared *The 10-Week Flexible Investment Plan: A beginner's guide to stock market success.* To understand what the book will do for you, first take in what it will not. No book in itself can make you into an investment genius. No book will have you investing like a professional from scratch after only a day or two of study, no matter what the expensive investment seminar leaders may tell you.

What *The 10-Week Flexible Investment Plan* will do is to give you a thorough and, I hope, enjoyable grounding in the basics of investing on the stock market. You will learn to adapt your investment techniques to suit your own needs, and market conditions. *Global-investor.com* has included me in its highly acclaimed book of investing rules as one of the 150 leading financial experts in the world. Let me pass on to you the fruits of my experience.

This book will work for you either as a standalone course, or, if you have access to the Internet, in conjunction with my Web site. I have established for you a unique flexi-program which is divided into 10 sections, each of which is designed to take up a week of your time (some of your evenings and weekend time only). Take this course slowly, and as you read, have a highlighter pen in your hand to underline important points.

Do attempt the Investor Power Quiz at the end of each section. As you try to answer the questions, you will be reinforcing in your mind what you have read. This will help you in your own investing. I have used the quiz technique effectively as a tutor and course material writer on the market-leading investment course that is published by Fleet Street Group. Reap the benefits of my proven approach.

I expect that you will gain from this book a sense of the excitement, the thrills, and the danger of the stock market. If you start investing in the right spirit, and learn from your mistakes, do not be surprised if you become highly successful financially.

You should also enjoy the challenge. That is important. Everybody I know who makes money out of the stock market loves it. Your enthusiasm, if channelled effectively using the techniques described in the following pages, really *can* take you a long way. The value investing principles that I recommend in this book have worked well for many in the past.

Please note, however, that nothing is infallible. No method works equally well for everybody at any given time. Part of your investment education is undoubtedly that you must take responsibility for your own decisions. You will always invest your money at your *own* risk.

With the risk of losing everything, which serious stock market investors incur, comes potential unlimited reward. It is a heady combination. Through this book, I will give you a friendly helping hand in narrowing the odds. Enough now of the preliminaries. I will step aside, and leave you to enjoy the show. . .

Your investment strategy

Your flexi-program

In this crucial first week of your flexi-program, you will discover why it is important to invest flexibly on the stock market, and how you should go about this. We will take an overview of the stock market and how it works, covering some of the material that investors want to know but are afraid to ask. This chapter is the rock on which the rest of your knowledge will be built. Relax and enjoy reading it.

First steps

First get your finances in order

Canny investors who make money from our flexible methods of investing on the stock market already have a pension, life assurance, and rainy day money – perhaps £5,000 stashed in the highest interest account that they can find.

With these staple investments in place, our kind of investors are focusing almost exclusively on investing in shares. Partly because so many of them are, or have been, City professionals, they are far more successful at the game than most.

Beyond this, these investors who use our methods differ. Some are cautious, others are bold. They are all prepared to buy the right shares and hold, which makes them investors, but some also like to buy and sell within a few weeks, or days, or hours. This makes them traders.

All users of our strategies use fundamental analysis. This involves stock-picking on the basis of ratio analysis, using numbers in the report and accounts. Some also (but never as a substitute) use technical analysis, which involves analysing charts to forecast future stock price movements.

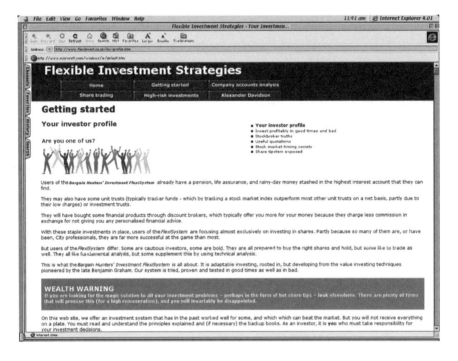

Figure 1.1 Investment basics

Your key to success

In the main, you will be investing for the medium to long term. This means that, if the price fluctuates, you will not be selling out in a panic. Nor will you be taking your profits in a rush.

As an alternative – or simultaneous – strategy, you may become a trader. On this basis, you will buy and resell shares quickly, within a short time period. The high losses that many traders suffered in the aftermath of the high-tech stock meltdown from March 2000 have demonstrated the risks. We will look at trading in detail in Week 7.

Why you need to be flexible

Time and time again, the biggest mistake the starting investor makes is a lack of flexibility. This shows itself when he or she invests in stocks which, while cheap on fundamentals, decline in value if the underlying company is in trouble. It shows itself too in blind investment in high-tech stocks that are trading far above fair valuation.

Most dangerously of all, private investors sometimes get stuck with a losing stock for the wrong reasons, such as loyalty or familiarity. If the stock is on a serious decline, sell out.

Your choice of broker

It is not just in stock selection that investors must be flexible. It is also in choice of brokers, and methods of investing.

If, for instance, you have an advisory broker who is losing you money, it is human nature – particularly if you are kind hearted – to give that person one more chance, as you justify it to yourself, to recoup the losses that he or she made you earlier. Perhaps also, in your heart of hearts, you cannot be bothered to change brokers.

To start using an online broker – where you make your own decisions, and nobody is holding your hand – is not an easy step. Still harder is it to change your online broker for another that is cheaper, more efficient, or more geared towards your needs. I guess that as human beings we are quite loyal by nature, and quite lazy. We also fear the unknown. In my 25 odd years of fully adult life, I have come across many investors. The more flexible they are, the more likely they are to rectify and learn from investing mistakes, and to make money on the stock market instead of losing it.

Unfortunately, flexibility is not a quality that stockbrokers encourage in their clients. They like to see the losers coming back for more. Remember, the stockbrokers make money when you invest, regardless of whether you make money or not.

Think flexibly

Think flexibly, and you can make money on the market. It sounds easy but, in practice, it isn't. Allow yourself to be a child again, and allow your thoughts to wander, providing one possibility after another. Above all, be independent in your investment thinking.

Every great investor has ultimately evolved his or her own methods of investing by such trial and error. You must do the same. Help is at hand, initially from this book, and also from my Web site Flexible Investment Strategies. If you have access to the Internet, visit it now at www.flexinvest.co.uk.

It is a result of this Web site that the need for this book became glaringly obvious. The flexible investment strategies that have worked so well for the City professionals – my colleagues – in their private investing, can also work for you.

Become self-reliant

As an investor in the stock market, you must become self-reliant. This means you must learn to pick stocks. You must also buy and sell at the right time, and take responsibility for your mistakes.

Until you are able to do this, you will be at the mercy of a small army of brokers, tipsters and others who want your money. But it is time now for some more specific investment education. Let's start with the basics.

What are shares?

If you buy ordinary shares – which are what people usually mean when they talk about shares – you are buying a stake in a company, or, as some prefer to put it, a unit in a stock.

Stocks are often traded on an exchange and can go up or down in value, which is reflected in a fluctuating share price. The selling price is slightly less than the mid-price level, and the buying price is slightly more. The difference between the selling and buying price is the spread.

Play the shareholder's game

By owning a share, you are a part-owner of the company, and may attend an annual general meeting (AGM). You also have voting rights. If you do not hold the shares through a nominee account, you have the right to receive an annual report and accounts and full shareholder perks. Today, nominee accounts are becoming the norm, and are very convenient, but they limit your rights.

Beat the market average

As a shareholder, you can sell your shares for the current market price at any time (except if the shares are suspended). If you prefer, you can simply hold your shares in the hope that they will rise in value, and the dividend, if any, will rise too. The FTSE All Share index, which represents the 900 largest shares on the London Stock Exchange, has historically given investors an average 8 per cent real return, taken over a long average.

If you can beat this, you will be doing excellently, as most fund managers fail to do so, when expenses for investing in these funds are taken into account. If you invest in the right shares in the right time, you may double your money or more, but you must counter-balance such gains with the losses from failed investments.

A share that is a loser one day may be a winner the next. But do not bank on this as shares often follow trends. If a share has been a steady loser – or winner – for some months, it is more likely than not to continue to do so.

The value of dividends

Many companies quoted on the markets pay a dividend, typically twice-yearly, which represents a pay out from profits to shareholders. The share price goes up a little as the so-called Dividend Day approaches, and then falls when the shares become categorized as ex-dividend (after the dividend has been distributed).

Small growth companies often do not pay a dividend, but this is not necessarily a bad thing. They plough earnings back into the business, instead of paying it out in the form of dividends to share-holders. If a company grows fast, the capital gain arising from a soaring share price can more than compensate for the lack of dividend.

Diversification

If you are a beginner, the conventional wisdom is that you should diversify your share portfolio. This means that you will invest in say five companies or more, not in the same sector, each in a different one. The obvious advantage is that, if one share falls in value, another may outperform, so balancing out the portfolio's overall performance.

But flexible investors – particularly when they have had a little experience – know that it sometimes pays to break the rules. Once diversification gets too much, it weakens the performance of the portfolio as there are too many shares in it. The mediocre shares may drag down the winners.

The message is clear. If you have found what you think is a winning stock, it can often pay to invest exclusively in it, although, of course, the risks are greater than from investing in a diversified portfolio.

Blue chips – no longer so safe

Until the mid-1980s, the safe way to play the stock market was to invest in the large, long-established companies included in the FTSE 100 index, which has the 100 largest companies in the UK. Such an investment strategy still gives an element of security as large companies are unlikely to go bust overnight, and have greater negotiating power when it comes to gaining extra finance to expand or stay afloat.

These FTSE 100 companies are known as blue chips. The market capitalization, which is the share price multiplied by the number of shares in issue, might be several billion pounds or more. Among blue chip companies that I like right now is Lloyds Bank, which is committed to creating shareholder value. This in practice means cutting costs and enhancing earnings. I also like Vodafone, an international mobile telephone group, and Glaxo Wellcome, the drugs giant.

What do these companies have in common? They are all market leaders. At the time of writing, they are looking quite cheap as the stock market is depressed. They all have some defensive qualities.

As any investor should, I reserve the right to change my mind. In recent years, some blue chips have severely underperformed. In particular, some high-tech companies included in the FTSE 100 index have in some cases done badly because the share price soared briefly far higher than the fundamentals justified.

ARM Holdings, the computer chip maker, was one of the casualties, although this is a market-leading company and will survive. There have also been poor performers from the old economy (stable industries such as manufacturing, oil and conventional retailing), particularly when the sector is out of favour.

A mock blue chip portfolio

Before we go any further, let's create an imaginary portfolio of five blue chips for you. This will illustrate the process and benefits of diversification. Let's first suppose that you intend to invest in telephone group BT, as you believe that the company has restructured itself and has prospects. That is fine, but the telecommunications sector can move in and out of favour quickly.

As a sensible investor, therefore, you would like to invest also in other sectors to diversify your risk. You might like retailing, which generates cash quickly, although the profit margins are low. You will invest in Safeway, which gives you a stake in a major food retailer.

As a defensive measure, you will invest in a clearing bank. The share price is likely to remain buoyant in times of recession, assuming that the bank is not exposed to too many bad loans. You may decide on Barclays.

You will also invest in ARM Holdings, which is firmly in the area of high-tech stocks. This is for a little bit of fast upward potential. The flip side is that the stock may plummet, but you can hope that your other holdings will then remain steady. Finally, at times when the oil price is looking positive, you might want to invest in a diversified oil group such as Shell.

This portfolio consists entirely of blue chip stocks, and so, within the equities arena, is medium rather than high risk. You could spice up your activity by diversifying into risky small company shares (see below, and Week 6) as part of the overall portfolio. At the other extreme, you could reduce the risk by diversifying from exclusively equities into bonds.

Smaller sized companies

Below the FTSE 100 index comes the FTSE 250 index. In this are included the next largest companies on the London Stock Market. They are large enough to survive some hard times, but have more room for growth than the very large blue chips.

Companies that are too small to be included in the FTSE 100 or the FTSE 250 (known together as the FTSE 350) may be in the Small Companies Index. This consists of all companies outside the FTSE 350 that are included in the FTSE All Share index.

Below this, is the FTSE Fledgling index, which consists of companies too small to be included in the All Share. These are still companies that have achieved a full listing on the London Stock Exchange. The market capitalization of such companies can theoretically be as little as £700,000, but it is usually at least a few million pounds.

Next down the scale comes the Alternative Investment Market (AIM). Here many small companies, typically with a market capitalization of between £1 million and £30 million, make a debut. Requirements for being quoted on the AIM are laxer than for being listed on the main market, and AIM stocks tend to be volatile. The best are high-flyers that may return investors many times their money. Some AIM stocks advance to a full listing.

Even riskier are shares listed on OFEX, which stands for off exchange. This is a market for unquoted stocks. Some of these companies go bust, and others lack liquidity, which means it is hard to sell the shares (although not always so hard to buy them). Nonetheless a few OFEX-listed shares do well, and may proceed to an AIM quotation or full listing. OFEX is run professionally and – very importantly – ethically, by a single market maker, JP Jenkins.

Where smaller companies fit into your portfolio

Although blue chip companies should be the staple of your portfolio, amounting to perhaps 50 per cent of your total shareholdings, it will benefit from the selective inclusion of small growth companies. This gives you diversification by size, which helps to balance your investment risk.

In the small companies field, be wary. There are a few winners and many losers, and the sector has recently sustained some years of underperformance. This is understandable as there is not the same level of buying interest as for larger companies. Fund managers are the country's largest investors as they buy shares for pension funds, unit trusts, insurance products, and similar. They ignore the tiddlers because they are hard to buy and sell in large quantities, and so the shares do not benefit from these major investors' buying support.

For this reason banks and stockbrokers research small stocks less. So small stocks are neglected, which throws up some real bargains for private investors, but not as many as you might think.

The techMark index

To acknowledge the new economy, the techMark index was created in 1999. This cuts across other indices to include innovative growth companies quoted on the London Stock Exchange. These companies are of all sizes and some have a very short track record.

If you are to invest heavily in high-tech stocks, you need to be especially flexible. Valuations are more flexible, and the stock performance is more volatile. It is often best to trade these stocks, rather than invest in them for the long term. For more on share trading, see Week 7.

Think internationally

Nowadays, with the advent of Internet investing, it is easier to invest internationally. Start by investing in UK stocks. Later, think about investing in Western Europe and the United States. You can deal in these stocks easily and cheaply through some brokers, and it helps to diversify your portfolio.

The biggest money from international investing comes from the less well established stock markets, such as in Russia or Poland. These are also the riskiest. I am particularly keen on the Russian stock market, where I have noticed some phenomenal investment bargains arising over the last couple of years. At the time of writing, Russia has stocks that trade at an 80 per cent share price discount to their Western and US peers, in sectors that range from oil to telecoms to other consumer goods.

This discount reflects what professional investors glibly describe as 'Russian risk'. As yet, Russian companies do not always have international accounts, and their standards of corporate governance can be inadequate. Some are poor at investor relations. The older companies may employ managers who are more interested in filtering money out of the company for their own purposes than paying a good dividend, or enhancing shareholder value. But some Russian companies, particularly if established in the post-Soviet era, are very Westernized in their thinking.

Why a stock price goes up or down

Whether a stock is fully listed, or quoted on a smaller exchange, in this country or abroad, its price goes up or down as a result of trading volume. The larger companies have much more of this than their smaller counterparts. They are highly liquid stocks.

Some investors clinically plan their investing, and buy stocks at bargain prices at the right time. Others buy and sell, less reliably in my view, on the basis of charts showing the past performance of charts and indices. For about this process, which is known as technical analysis, see Week 8.

The majority of investors base their investment decisions on short-term factors such as news events, growth forecasts, and – most commonly of all – rumours. Bear in mind that the market typically overreacts. If good news comes, the company's share price tends to rise too high. With bad news, it falls too far.

These overreactions will correct themselves, but not for hours, days, or even weeks or months. If you are quick off the mark, there is time for you to exploit the price differential and to sell a temporarily overvalued share, or buy an undervalued one. Such timing apart, you should be looking for stocks that offer value on fundamentals.

Analysts get it wrong

As an investor, you must aim to select stocks that beat the market average over a period. To achieve this, you must develop your own stock-picking skills. Do not take analysts at face value. In practice, they sometimes make serious mistakes. They are also often biased in a company's favour, particularly if their firm is conducting corporate business for it, or hopes to.

Unsurprisingly in the circumstances, analysts try to give a stock a Buy or Hold recommendation, rather than a Sell. They also don't want to offend the companies involved and, besides, need to generate orders for their firm's sales team. Institutional investors know how to read between the lines.

Proponents of the efficient market theory believe that it is impossible to beat the market average except by a fluke. This is on the basis that the share price reflects all that becomes known about any given stock. The famous random walk theory, which is a version of this, suggests that if you are blindfolded and pick out stocks with a pin from the list in your newspaper, you will create a portfolio that does at least as well as those run by most fund managers.

Fortunately for serious investors, the efficient market theory is not true. Warren Buffett, the Omaha-based billionaire, is the most successful of the many investors who have proved this. Except for a few glitches *en route*, he has consistently beaten the market average. You should aim to do the same in your own investing.

Collective investments

If you want to reduce your investment risk by diversifying, but don't trust yourself yet (notice I say 'yet') to buy shares directly, I recommend that you buy collective investments. These reduce your risk by investing in a wide range of equities, as well as sometimes in fixed-income instruments, and in property.

First, consider a unit trust. This is an open-ended investment, which allows units in the fund to be enhanced or reduced in number as investors buy or sell. Selecting your unit trust requires judgement. The problem is that the vast majority of unit trusts underperform the market average, when all costs are taken into account. I suggest one of two routes.

First, try to select one of the relatively few high-fliers. Look for a unit trust that has been in the top quartile of its sector in terms of performance over the last three or five years. You will find the comparables in *Money Management*, or through various online sources. Look for the lowest possible management fees, and a fund manager with a proven track record. If this individual leaves, consider joining him or her at the new fund, rather than leaving your money in the one he or she has just left.

As an alternative, invest in a tracker fund. These are unit trusts that simply track the stock market – usually the FTSE 100 index, or the All Share index (the better performer in the past). Tracker funds have generally beaten most actively managed funds over a period, when costs are taken into account, although in recent years they have gone through a spell of underperformance. The charges are, in most cases, much lower than for actively managed funds.

Investment trusts, which are closed-ended funds held by vehicles quoted on the stock market, are cheaper for investors than unit trusts, and over some periods tend to have higher returns. The trusts are not allowed, as unit trusts are, to advertise or use financial advisers, and they pass on the cost savings to you as an investor.

Time to buy

Buy your chosen collective investment from a discount broker – if it has it on offer. The broker will give you a rebate on some of the up-front commission in return for not receiving advice. This way, you will pay a reduced price.

Otherwise, you can buy with a reduced up-front charge from a fund supermarket (as opposed to a mere brochure distributor) on the Internet.

The next step

Let's round off this section with a short quiz that will reveal what kind of investor you are. In preparing this quiz, I have adapted and expanded an earlier version which has proved enormously popular with users of my Web site. The quiz will help you find your own best approach to investment, and to plan your strategy with the necessary flexibility.

Investor power quiz

Answer each question with one of the three alternatives. Do not think too long, but respond as comes to mind.

1. If you invest money in the stock market, do you expect:
    (c) To lose everything because the stock market is difficult to understand, and the private investor does not really stand much chance.
    (a) To get it right and make a lot of money all at once.
    (b) To start making money sometimes, but to lose as well.

2. If you have invested money in shares, and the market suddenly plunges, do you:
    (a) Enjoy the rollercoaster ride and look for trading opportunities.
    (b) Keep an eye on your shares and if they are falling fast, cut your losses and sell them to free up capital for better investments.

(c) Decide that your worst fears are confirmed. You will never invest in the stock market again.

3. How much of your capital should you have on the stock market at any given time?
    (b) Some of your savings, after emergency money, insurance, pension, and perhaps bonds.
    (c) At most, only a tiny sum, perhaps £500 or £1,000. This represents fun money that you can afford to lose. In your view, the stock market is gambling.
    (a) Your life savings. They are better invested in the market than sitting in your building society.

4. As an investor, do you think you should:
    (b) Choose your investments with a little help from your broker.
    (a) choose your own investments, even if this means making a mistake.
    (c) Leave it to your broker to decide. That's the broker's job. If you're using a professional, he or she must know what he or she is doing.

5. Do you like to research an opportunity before you take it up:
    (a) Never. I prefer to act on instinct.
    (c) Yes, but often as an escape from taking action.
    (b) Up to a point.

6. If you inherited £250,000, would you prefer to:
    (b) Invest it in the stock market.
    (c) Put the money in the bank (and maybe some of it under the mattress).
    (a) Invest in a race horse.

7. For the next five years of your life, do you:
    (b) Have hazy plans.
    (a) Try to set goals.
    (c) Take the view that to plan so far ahead is pointless.

8. In your life, do you like:
    (c) Absolute certainty.
    (a) Plenty of uncertainty, and the flexibility that comes with it.
    (b) Certainty of course, but spiced with a little of the unknown.

9. Are you the type of person who:
   (b) Likes to make your own financial decisions, but with some guidance from professionals.
   (a) Prefers to make completely independent financial decisions.
   (c) Feels safer if a professional always makes financial decisions.

10. Let's suppose that you have shares in a risky biotechnology company. If its key product is suddenly proved faulty and has to be withdrawn, with the result that the share price falls 80 per cent in a day, do you:
    (c) Get furious and take your money out of equities altogether.
    (b) Take your money out of equities for a while.
    (a) Vow to choose your next speculative stock more carefully, and sell it at the first sign of trouble.

11. You are invested in a number of safe but dull companies that have performed only in line with the market. You feel:
    (a) Furious. You've played it too safe.
    (b) That you've nothing to complain about, but, next time, you might include some higher risk stocks in your portfolio.
    (c) That the portfolio might not work so well again. You will cash in and put the money in a high interest account.

12. Do you prefer to hold your money:
    (c) In cash.
    (a) In high-risk, growth companies.
    (b) In blue chip shares.

13. You have inherited £100,000. Which would you prefer?
    (c) Stick the money in your piggy bank where you can keep an eye on it.
    (a) Invest in a range of shares.
    (b) Invest some of the cash in shares and keep the rest in a safer place.

14. If you see the share price of an exciting but unprofitable young high-tech company rising, would you invest?
    (c) No. The risk is too great.
    (a) Yes. You'll put all your spare money on this and hope to make a killing.

(b) Up to a point. You'll put only a little money into the company.

15. If the market is rising fast, what will you do with your winning stocks?
    (c) Sell quickly. Profits are not real until they are converted into cash.
    (b) Keep the shares and sell at the first sign of downturn.
    (a) Increase your holdings in the shares.

So how did you score?

Results

Mostly (a)s
You are a confident but potentially reckless investor.
You are a very confident investor, but do not always think before you act. You are good at taking risks, but this means that you can lose money as well as make it. You may make a killing from investing in shares during a roaring bull market. But you may lose everything by taking foolhardy risks when market conditions are dangerous. As a strategy, you must spend longer researching stocks and planning your investments.

Mostly (b)s
You are a cautious but willing investor.
You are cautious but willing to invest, which can be a powerful combination. Unfortunately, you do not always get the balance right. You will improve with practical experience. Sometimes also, you will lack flair in the stock-picking game, and this may prevent you from joining the ranks of the top investors.

Mostly (c)s
You are an excessively cautious investor.
You are excessively cautious and need to have more confidence in your own judgement. Read and learn more about the stock market. Then select a stock or two, perhaps with your broker's help, and invest. You will make some mistakes, but, if you learn from these, you will improve.

How to select and use your broker

Your flexi-program

This week, we will look at online, advisory and discretionary brokers. We will also see how the dubious firms operate.

By the end of this week, you will know how to distinguish between the various brokers, and how to get the best out of your chosen firm.

Online brokers

Introduction

I favour online brokers, so I am going to tell you about these first. In almost every case, they are execution-only, which means they leave you to make the crucial investment decisions. This way, you may make mistakes, but you will be, at least, captain of your own ship.

Get started

To open your online account, you will need to download a form from a broker's Web site, or request a form to be sent to you by e-mail. Print this off, and fill it in by hand. Send this to the broker, with cash – usually at least £1,000 – to open your account. The firm will hold this money in an interest-paying account until you make your first trade.

Choose the right broker

The online brokers in the UK operate with different cost structures and services. Some simply have a glorified e-mail service. You can buy or sell shares through such brokers by issuing your instructions by e-mail. This is a slow way to deal. Avoid these brokers, unless you deal only very occasionally.

Most usual is the browser-based broker, such as Charles Schwab. Through such firms, you can execute a trade yourself, rather than ask the broker to do it for you. You can deal at a price shown on screen through a connection with the London Stock Exchange.

Browser-based brokers can be quite slow when Internet traffic is slow. If you are an active trader, avoid them. Go instead for an active trader broker. Buying or selling through such a firm can be expensive, but it is fast. An active trader broker provides software that you can load on to your computer. This software will evaluate a portfolio and construct charts, also enabling fast trade execution. The firm will not ask for order confirmation, as some browser-based brokers do.

As a routine, the prices at which you may deal in a stock are quoted on a bid-offer basis. 'Bid' means the price at which you can sell, and 'offer' the price at which you can buy. A broker will sometimes have only one or the other. When the two are put together, this is known as the spread. For example, a spread of 8–10 means that you can sell at 8p or buy at 10p.

Your broker will deal with market makers. These are the firms that buy and sell shares on a wholesale basis, dealing with the brokers. To confuse matters, sometimes a market maker and broker are the same firm, although, in such cases, so-called Chinese walls are supposed to exist, preventing conflicts of interest.

The full range of bid and offer prices that market makers are offering in a stock are made available to investors through Level 11 data. The screen-based services that provide this also show when a market maker changes its prices. If you have access, you can note the level of demand for a stock beyond the best bid and ask prices, which will show you how much resistance there is to price changes.

Back-up is useful

Computers sometimes crash, and back-up will be useful. If your broker offers a telephone dealing service for this purpose, so much

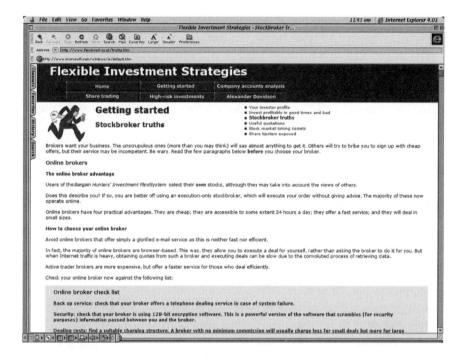

Figure 2.1 Stockbroker truths

the better. As an alternative, you can open a back-up account with another broker. Please note, however, that although you can use such an account easily for buying shares, it is not so easy if you sell this way.

If you hold your shares through nominee holdings with one broker, you will need to make a transfer so that you can sell them through another. This is expensive and inconvenient. The issue does not apply if you hold share certificates in a stock, which are in hard copy form only, and are sent to you in the post. But these days, brokers like share certificates increasingly less.

Cheapest is not always best

Choose a broker with the right cost structure for your needs. If the firm has no minimum charge, it will probably charge less for small deals but more for larger ones. This is ideal if you invest in small amounts. If, however, you invest with large sums, you will be better off using a broker that will operate more cheaply for this purpose. Such a broker is likely to have a substantial minimum charge.

The very cheapest brokers may deal only at specified times in the day, putting all the trades together. This way, they cut costs and pass the savings on to you, but you will have to take pot luck on how the price has moved in the interim. Avoid this situation unless you are an occasional investor.

Note that some firms charge for such services as having an account or processing share certificates.

Special services

Some brokers offer paper trading or demos as an initial substitute for trading. Many brokers offer research and news services online, but such facilities are available free on the Web, including with other brokers.

Sometimes, your online broker gives you access to new equity issues. We will cover this interesting area of investing in Week 5. The golden rule is, avoid most new issues in a bear market, but buy in a bull market. Be prepared to sell shortly after the stock has come to market, as any immediate rise may be sadly temporary.

Security

Your broker will use encryption software, to ensure that the information passed between his or her firm and yourself online is scrambled, and so inaccessible to thieves. This software should be 128-bit encryption, which is the strongest kind. Your broker should also hold insurance to protect client accounts in case it should run into financial problems.

To use your broker's services, you will be issued with a password. Keep this absolutely secret and use it when you're not being watched. To protect your privacy further, make your password a complicated nonsense word. Do not leave your computer without switching off when you are in the secure part of your broker's Web site. When you have completed a transaction, print off evidence of it, and log out correctly.

The mechanics of dealing

Look up the EPIC code (a three or four letter symbol) for the stock which interests you. This is usually possible on your broker's Web site. You can find dealing prices on the screen of your online broker.

You can deal in quoted shares in at least the normal market maker size (NMS). This represents the minimum number of shares for which a market maker must quote firm bid and offer prices. The smaller the stock, the smaller the NMS tends to be, and the wider the spread. The market maker maintains this position because small stocks can be hard to buy and sell. To read more about small company investing, see Week 6.

How to buy US shares online

If you want to buy US shares online, choose a broker which will deal for you at a low commission. If you are prepared to deposit a signifi-cant sum up front, you can use a US online broker.

To register with US online dealers, you will often find the registra-tion forms online. Print your form off, fill it out, and send it to the broker by snail (ordinary) mail. Include up-front funds as required, in US currency.

As an investor in US shares, you will be taking a risk on the sterling/dollar exchange rate, but the bid-offer spread is usually lower than in the UK, and you will pay no stamp duty.

From the perspective of the US tax authorities, you will be a non-resident alien. For this reason, you must complete a W-8 form, which is a certificate of foreign status. You can download this from the Web site of the US Internal Revenue Service. Send it to your broker.

For some useful guidance on investing in the US high-tech market, go to the Web site of Nasdaq (www.nasdaq.co.uk). Also, visit the US Web site of The Motley Fool (www.fool.com), which gives valuable, reader-friendly investment advice.

Place your order

I recommend that, if your broker allows it, you set a limit order. This means that, if the order is not fulfilled with the price that you have specified, it is cancelled. Some brokers accept limit orders that they keep open for the day, cancelling if they cannot fulfil them. Others either execute the limit order immediately, or cancel it.

If you do not specify a limit order, you will buy at best, which means the best price in the market. This way, you may pay a higher price than you expected if the market has moved against you since you placed the order.

When you place your order, avoid making mistakes. If you order 30,000 shares when you had intended 3,000, you will be liable for these. But in case you make such an error, inform your broker immediately. He will usually at least do a cancelling trade, which will minimize your losses.

If you do not yet feel confident about making your own investment decisions, or haven't the time, consider using an advisory broker. If so, my advice is that you should be wary. The good ones are fewer than you may think.

Advisory brokers

Truth is, advisory brokers often know little. Many come from backgrounds unrelated to financial services. I personally know brokers who had until recently been bartenders, timeshare salespeople, shop assistants, burger bar waiters, or simply off the dole queue. These are often nice people, and you have to admire their opportunism. But when you see them making a fortune from trading shares with private clients, you can't help wondering if it is not a little too easy to become a stockbroker. What are the requirements?

Nowadays, stockbrokers need to pass the Registered Persons exam. This is a very simple multiple choice paper, and if the broker holds it, this doesn't mean he or she knows much. I have in the past done this exam, and passed it, three times, to keep up to date with the basics. You forget the stuff quickly.

I also hold the Securities Institute Diploma, which is sometimes represented as the highest qualification in the securities industry. To pass this exam requires two years' study. Again, it is a limited qualification. Some of the reading required is as basic as scanning the *Financial Times* several weeks before sitting the exam.

The least well-informed in the stockbroking profession tend to be the half-commission brokers, so-called because they split commissions earned (perhaps on a 30–70 basis) with their firm. Some of these brokers obtain their share know-how second-hand, either from old research reports of other firms or, still less reliably, from press tips.

If you are prepared to risk using an advisory broker, look for know-how and genuine experience in the individual who deals with you personally, and not just his or her firm. Also look at the level of the individual's service. If you have less than £50,000 to invest, you may find it hard to get a good London broker, although there are no firm rules. A provincial broker may give you a more personal service. The firm will probably have more time for you than its London counter-part, and will probably be a bit cheaper.

Watch for warning signs

In the UK, brokers are usually regulated and are accountable for their actions under the Financial Services Act (FSA). In practice, it is usually difficult and expensive to pursue the wrongdoers.

Don't get caught in the first place. Watch for signs of dubious activity, or simply ignorance, in your broker. If the wrong kind of broker does not know the answer to your questions, he or she will never admit this. Instead you might be told: 'Hang on please, I've just got a call coming in from the States.' The broker will then put you on hold while he or she checks your query and then returns to you with: 'Sorry about that. What was your question?' You will repeat it, and the broker will provide the right answer as if spontaneously.

Alternatively, the broker may avoid the question altogether. If you ask for a company's latest earnings, he or she may say: 'That's unimportant for the company at this stage. What counts is revenue.'

The dubious broker's sales pitch

Dubious advisory brokers represent the stock they are pushing as special, and the market as always rising. At the same time, these brokers cover their position. They never say that a stock will, or is certain to, rise in value. Instead, they say that it should, or is likely to do so. This way, victims of their sales pitch will later find it much harder to accuse them of giving misleading information.

Brokers may also cover themselves by saying something like: 'Of course, I can't make any guarantees about any stock – you under-stand that?' and pause for the client's consent (recorded on tape), before continuing with their exaggerated claims. Clients appreciate the apparent sincerity.

Dubious brokers present news and research selectively to back their sales case. If a stock has performed poorly, they will say that it is under-valued, and stress the benefits of a low PE ratio. But if they are selling a growth stock with a high PE ratio, brokers will stress the benefits of relative strength (a share price that outperforms the market).

Keeping control

Dubious advisory brokers prefer you not to sell, unless you reinvest the proceeds into shares that you buy from them. They want to keep control over your money. One broker responds to selling clients as follows: 'You must be out of your mind. You should be buying more.' Weak clients may then be persuaded to double up their holdings.

The broker also sometimes says: 'Don't sell that one' implying without justification that he or she knows of major developments within the company. But if the broker keeps the comments vague, you cannot later accuse him or her of specific misleading statements.

If you prove insistent on selling, the broker may ask you to wait for just another couple of weeks – during which, he or she suggests, the company's fortunes may take a turn for the better. If you agree, the broker knows that, after a few days, you will very likely no longer feel such a pressing need to sell. As an additional disincentive, the broker may put the onus on you to ring him or her.

Sell stock to reinvest

Dubious brokers will churn your portfolio, which means that they will buy and sell shares for you with the sole aim of generating commission for themselves. Churning is in breach of the Financial Services Act, but it goes on all the time. The disguised churn gives the broker an easy loophole. Here, the broker manipulates private investors into making what they think is their own decision to sell part of their portfolio and use the proceeds to buy new shares.

The broker will say something like: 'Of course I couldn't recom-mend that you sell your blue chip shares to release capital for investing in this high-tech stock, but I know what I would do in your position.'

I know of one broker who uses such manipulative techniques. He once regularly churned the portfolio of a school-dinner lady who had inherited some money for investing. She invested over £100,000 with him in high-risk unquoted stocks, and, over a few months, although in bull market conditions, lost almost every penny.

The share pushers

The biggest danger is from pushers of unquoted stocks. These opportunists operate by telephone and on the Internet, selling to unsuspecting, usually inexperienced private investors. If you invest in the stocks that they offer you, you will usually lose all your money. It rarely takes long.

The US Securities and Exchange Commission has demonstrated the risks through a startlingly authentic Internet hoax campaign designed to show the investing public how easily the fraudulent share pushers may dupe them. The Commission, which supervises the US securities industry, established a trick Web address at www. mcwhortle.com. Go to this address and take a look. The site represents McWhortle as an established and well-known manufacturer of biological defense mechanisms.

Visitors to the Web site are apparently encouraged to apply for shares in McWhortle through an international public offering, and to send in their cheques. As they proceed, they are led to a page that reads: 'If you responded to an investment like this...You could get scammed.'

On this site, you will find marvellously convincing promotional material that shows how convincingly a fraudulent company can market itself – at least to naïve investors who cannot – or will not – check the financial statements.

For news and insights on fraudulent share pushing activity in general, visit Stock Detective, a US-based vigilant Web site that is now based at www.financialweb.com/skdindex.asp. It exposes scams across the world, but particularly in the United States and Canada.

If you are an active private investor who gives out your telephone number, you will probably be pestered by pushers of such high risk stocks and worse. They will have obtained your name from lists of active investors that are rented out on a regular basis.

If operating from abroad, these share pushers often use switching offices. By this means, they will be working in a secret office in one country, while their letterhead and phone number will suggest that they are based in another. This will mislead the majority of investors.

In such cases, the salesperson – who is typically operating under a false name – prefers not to give you a phone number. He or she likes instead to initiate the calls. If, however, you do call, the receptionist who answers will say that the salesperson is unavailable. He or she will pass on a message, in reality to the other office.

Many of the dubious salespeople earn high commissions for the risks that they take – typically 10 per cent on all revenues from stocks that they sell, and maybe as much as 60 per cent. The shares are usually in unknown, unquoted companies, or represented as being in blue chips. In either case, you are in reality buying nothing.

The salesperson will do a first deal with you, then pass your details to a so-called loader, who tries to sell more shares to you. Some of these companies sell shares via the Internet as well. Their Web sites are often highly plausible.

Pump-and-dump

Even if the shares are real, you can be set up. In the pump-and-dump routine, the promoters buy huge quantities of stock cheap under nominee names, then create demand by hard-selling the stock intensively. When the share price is at its highest, they sell out their own holdings at a fat profit. The share price tumbles, and small investors rush to sell.

Small stocks are typically illiquid in the best of cases, but they are invariably at their worst when associated with a pump-and-dump. The problem is that the shares are sellable, if at all, only in small sizes, with the gap between the bid and offer price being large. To find out more about how the pump-and-dump works, read my most recent novel *Stock Market Rollercoaster*. For more on this book, see Week 9.

A golden rule for dealing with the share sharks

If you are approached by one of the share sharks on the telephone, put down the receiver. Do not worry about being rude. It is not always easy to make, say, £50,000. It is very easy to lose it in a few telephone calls, or even in one. Do not become a victim of your own greed.

Rotten apples in every basket

Some individual brokers who learnt their trade in highly dubious firms are now operating in apparently respectable stockbrokers. They keep their jobs mainly because of the high level of business they bring in. The smaller an investor you are, the more likely you are to come across such a broker. Even if the individual is properly authorized, he or she may still be dubious. Remember that the securities industry regulates itself. As investment guru Robert Beckman once quipped, this is like getting Dracula to look after a blood bank.

Sometimes, the regulators draw the line and decline to authorize a dubious firm. In such a case, the firm often enters a drawn-out appeal. In the meantime, it claims a provisional or interim authorization, and carries on dealing, raking in as much money as possible from gullible private clients.

The regulators may give up. I have known key individuals from their number shift over to the worst of the firms that they are supposed to be regulating, enticed by a high financial package. I know of one regulator who did this, and became one of the core directors of a really crooked share-dealing firm.

Discretionary brokers

How discretionary brokers work

Discretionary brokers choose which shares to buy and sell on your behalf. They are most used when it comes to investing amounts over £100,000. I am sure that some of these brokers are wonderful. But so many have made a complete mess of private client portfolios that I really urge you to be really careful.

Be highly selective. Because a firm has a big name, it doesn't mean that it won't lose you 60 per cent or more of your money within a matter of months. What counts is the calibre of the individual who is handling your portfolio. Someone who has been successful in a roaring bull market may be terrible in a bear market.

If you want to hear a typical horror story, visit the Web site at www.mykillikaccount.co.uk, where investors explain how they have lost large sums of money investing with a leading broker.

If despite these caveats, you want to go ahead with a discretionary broker, please follow these simple rules. Watch what the broker is doing with your money. Query any transactions with which you do not feel comfortable. Discuss your portfolio with your broker.

As part of this process, ask for monthly – rather than quarterly or half-yearly – statements. This shows your broker that you take your money seriously. If you find he or she is losing you capital, do not hesitate to insist that he or she sells your shares and, for the time being, holds cash.

Your broker should be applying some kind of stop loss system, by which he or she sells shares if they fall below a certain percentage level. If this is not the case, make sure that he or she has an effective strategy for selling losers.

Settlement and nominee accounts

Once you have dealt, you will usually need to settle within three days. This is known as T+3. Settlement is electronic, through the Crest computerized system, which matches trades with payments and provides notice of changes to the share register. If, however, you have paper share certificates, you will settle within 10 days.

Online brokers prefer to hold your shares electronically, through a pooled nominee account. This way, you have your shares registered in the name of a nominee company run by your broker, but will retain beneficial ownership. However, you will forfeit the right to receive an annual report and accounts and full shareholder perks, including right to vote at shareholder meetings. You will still receive dividends and regular account statements.

Alternatively, you can have a Crest-sponsored member account. In this case, when you trade shares, it will be your details, and not your broker's, that are passed electronically with the transaction.

Complaints

If your broker has dealt with you incompetently or dishonestly, first complain to the firm. If this does not get a satisfactory result, complain to the regulators. At all times keep a record of deals, and of conversations.

An industry complaints bureau – arranged through the regulators – can mediate between the firm and yourself, and attempt to reach a resolution. If this fails, you can choose to go to arbitration, which is at the option of yourself as client, or take court action, but not both. In past disputes with a recalcitrant stockbroker, I have gone to mediation, and found this satisfactory, but only because I refused to accept the broker's first two settlement offers.

Alternatively, you can complain to the press about a firm. Go to quality national newspapers, where exposure will hit the firm hardest. Ideally choose Sunday papers where the journalists have more time to dig around.

Avoid tabloid newspapers, as they will often distort the information that you give them. I know of one investor who complained about a dishonest dealing firm to a well-known tabloid Sunday newspaper. His complaint was well-founded. The result was, however, appalling. The journalist persuaded the investor to have his photograph taken for the newspaper, and this was published. The investor was represented as motivated by greed and undeserving of sympathy, no less than the stockbroking firm that had cheated him.

I have known a number of people who have talked at length to tabloid newspaper journalists. An article has invariably appeared. These people without exception have told me that the experience has been one of the worst in their lives. The message is clear. Do not talk to a tabloid newspaper for any reason. If you do, expect trouble. Above all, never accept payment from such a newspaper as it may regard this as giving it *carte blanche* to say anything it likes about you.

If your stockbroker defaults, you will have access to the industry's compensation scheme. The first £30,000 of any proven claim will be met in full, and 90 per cent of the next £20,000 will be met – with £48,000 being the maximum compensation paid to any single claimant.

Investor power quiz

Now that we have covered the basics of choosing and using your stockbroker, try this quiz. Answer each of the following 10 questions, ticking only one of the three possible answers. Then check your score.

1. An online broker:
   (a) Operates via the Internet.
   (b) Specializes in fishing stocks.
   (c) Only deals in Internet and other high-tech stocks.

2. The fees of conventional advisory brokers are:
   (a) Higher than for online brokers because you are paying for advice.
   (b) Non-existent if you do enough deals.
   (c) Always lower than for online brokers.

3. Dubious stockbrokers offload shares through:
   (b) Small promotional cards inserted in cigarette packs.
   (c) Visiting you without an appointment.
   (a) Telephone and Internet.

4. Paper share certificates are:
   (a) No longer as popular as nominee accounts.
   (c) The most popular way now to hold your shares.
   (b) Typically worth more than the shares they represent.

5. A broker who holds a discretionary portfolio on your behalf:
   (a) Makes his or her own decisions on what stocks to buy and sell on your behalf, and when.
   (b) Will buy and sell individual shares for you only on your specific instructions.
   (c) Neither of the above.

6. Limit orders:
   (a) Set a limit on the price at which you will buy or sell shares.
   (c) Allow the broker to impose such a price limit at his or her discretion.
   (b) Are a large order that limits the liquidity of the underlying stock.

7. Online brokers always offer:
   (a) Facilities to obtain prices and to deal.
   (c) A significant online news and education service.
   (b) Analysts' research.

8. Advisory brokers have:
    (c) An accountancy or legal qualification in every case.
    (b) Five years' experience of working back office, as required, before they can deal with the public.
    (a) Industry qualifications in most cases, which are fairly basic compared to the requirements of solicitors, doctors and so on.

9. The pump-and-dump routine is:
    (a) A manoeuvre involving the sale of shares at a rising price that enables shareholders to sell out at a profit.
    (b) Plumbing facilities within broking firms.
    (c) The hiring and firing of brokers.

10. If you like to buy and sell shares in modest quantities, you will most easily find a suitable advisory broker:
    (b) Abroad.
    (c) In London.
    (a) In the provinces.

Answers

The correct answer is (a) in every case. Give yourself one mark for every correct answer. Now check the list below to see how you scored:

7–10. You have a good grasp of how brokers work. Use it to select the right broker for you. If it turns out to be the wrong choice, switch to another. Don't make the mistake of being loyal.

5–6. You have a fair understanding of brokers, but could benefit from reading this chapter again.

1–4. You don't yet have a good knowledge of the broking world, but no matter. Reread this chapter before you select (or change) your broker.

Make **money from interpreting financial statements**

Your flexi-program

With the collapse of Enron in January 2002, and the revelations of dubious accounting at Worldcom five months later, valuations of companies on the stock market have focused increasingly on old-fashioned fundamentals. Suddenly, ratio analysis, and scrutiny of the accounts are back in fashion.

As US fund manager and best-selling author John Train has argued, accounting is the language of business. If you are to understand the business in which you invest, you must understand the numbers. This way you will not be at the mercy of brokers and tipsters who recommend stocks without having good reason.

This week we will look at most of a report and accounts, including the profit & loss account and the balance sheet. We will leave the cash flow statement until Week 4. These are the three main components of a report and accounts, but there are plenty of others too. You need not just to read and interpret the accounts but also to calculate ratios. Pay particular attention to the boxed copy in this section headed Ratios Deciphered.

Do not feel discouraged if you do not take in everything included in Week 3 at once. This section and Week 4 are, in my view, the most important part of this course. You can – and should – revisit these pages at your leisure.

Some ground rules

What are accounts?

Most UK quoted companies issue accounts twice a year, including an interim statement after the first six months (the starting date will vary). This interim statement is not necessarily a pro rata indication of the full year profits.

Shortly after the full year, the company publishes full year figures, known as preliminaries. Next comes the full audited annual report and accounts, which provides a statement of the company's profits, its cash flow, and its financial position.

How do you get hold of a set of accounts?

To get hold of a set of accounts, telephone a company's registrar, and ask to be sent one. Alternatively, obtain a copy of the *Financial Times*, and telephone its free service for ordering company reports and accounts. If you want the accounts of a favoured company instantly, you can often download them from its own Web site.

Double-entry bookkeeping

Modern accounting is based on double-entry bookkeeping, which was invented at the end of the 15th century and first used in Italy. Under this system, any amount entered on the right side of one account, known as a credit, must be balanced by the same amount entered on the left side of another account, known as a debit. This way, it is possible to prepare a balance sheet with assets, or debit balances, equal to liabilities, or credit balances.

Double-entry bookkeeping is a mechanical exercise. I know as I have a professional qualification in it. Do not bother too much with this side of accounting. Instead, concentrate on interpreting the accounts.

Let's start reading the accounts

When I get a company report and accounts, I prefer to read it back-wards. This way, I see the numbers (at the back) first, which is the most important part. I see the glossy bits – which matter much less – last. But for the purposes of this chapter, we will look at the various parts approximately in order of presentation.

I also read different parts of the report and accounts in conjunction. If, for instance, profits (as on the profit & loss account) are good and cash flow (as on the cash flow statement) is bad, this starts a warning bell ringing. If I only considered profits, I would not notice this. In addition, I compare this year's figures with last year's. The two are always presented together.

Principles matter

All the financial statements have been put together on the basis of key principles.

Prudence
One key principle is prudence. Here, the company must report its numbers conservatively. Likely losses must be taken into the profit & loss account, but not likely gains. Potential bad debts must be written off immediately, and stock should be valued at the lower of cost or market value. If revenue is uncertain, it should be recognized only where collected in cash.

Accruals
Also note the accruals principle. Here, revenues and costs are matched regardless of timing. The profit & loss account (the statement covering a company's sales and profits or losses) includes income and expenditure at the time when the transaction took place. This is usually when it was invoiced, and not necessarily when cash is paid.

Consistency
Under the principle of consistency, a company should account for items in a consistent way from one year to the next. You can therefore safely compare a company's accounts this year with those in earlier years. There will be no unidentified changes in how the figures are presented.

Substance over form

Under the principle of substance over form, the accounts should reflect the commercial reality – and not just the legal form – of what has happened.

Going concern

Also, the report and accounts is prepared according to the principle of a going concern. It is assumed that the company will continue in business for the foreseeable future.

Materiality

Under the principle of materiality, anything material, and so potentially affecting users' decisions, must be disclosed in the accounts. Some accountants consider that if more than 5 per cent of the company is affected, this is material.

Let's get started

Now we will take a look at the report and accounts in more detail. If you want to learn at maximum speed, read the following pages in conjunction with a real report and accounts.

The financial statements

The chairman's statement

The chairman's statement at the front of the report and accounts – often written by the company's public relations team – will always represent the company in its best light. It will focus on the company's trading performance, its strategy and its prospects.

This statement is not subject to any auditing or accounting legislation, or even governed by a code of best practice. Despite this, the chairman should have considered his or her reputation in preparing the statement. If you read between the lines, you will often find valuable hints and perspectives on the company.

The directors' report

The directors' report helps you to interpret the numbers, and provides extra non-financial information. It includes details on dividend policy, and a business review, which, although limited so as not to reveal too much to competitors, can nonetheless say a fair bit. Post-balance sheet events are recorded.

The company's research and development (R&D) programme will be covered – if this is active, you want to see it turn into profits, so check the company's track record here. If R&D is being cut back, this will inflate short-term profits, but long-term development could suffer. Discover here too who are the company's major shareholders (holding 3 per cent or more). It will be worth taking note when they buy or sell shares in their own company.

Find out here too if the company has purchased its own shares, indicating it had no more profitable use for its spare cash. This increases the earnings per share (amount of profit attributable to every share) as, following the share buyback, the same level of earnings will be distributed among a smaller number of shareholders. The share price will usually have responded positively. Next year, the company may remain in favour as a result of the increased earnings per share, but this is uncertain. We will look at the earnings per share in more detail later in this section.

The operating and financial review

This statement is not mandatory but many companies have it. It provides more about the company's operations and identifies key future trends.

The profit & loss account

The profit & loss account is important as it is from this that the earnings per share, so highly regarded in the City, is culled. But never read this part of the financial statements in isolation. Profits can be high, but the company may be generating little cash. This is because of the flexible way in which profit may be defined. More about this later.

At this stage, let's take a quick look at a typical profit & loss account. In this mock example, x stands for a positive amount, and (x) for a negative amount.

UK profit & loss account:

Turnover	x
Cost of sales	(x)
	—
Gross profit	**x**
Administration costs	(x)
Distribution costs	(x)
Other operating income	x
	—
Operating profit	**x**
Profit on sale of fixed assets	x
Net interest payable	(x)
	—
Profit on ordinary activities before tax	x
Taxation on profit on ordinary activities	x
	—
Profit on ordinary activities after taxation	x
Minority interests	(x)
Dividend	(x)
	—
Retained profit for the financial year	**x**

Alternative layout

Here is a less common (alternative) layout for the top part of the profit & loss account, as far as operating profit:

Turnover	x
Raw materials	(x)
Staff costs	(x)
Change in stock and work-in-progress	(x)
Operating income	x
	—
Operating profit	x

Let us now look at the component parts of the profit & loss account (usual style) in more detail. I will include some items that do not always appear on the face of the profit & loss account. They may do so, or they may be in the notes to the accounts instead. These notes are situated at the back of the financial statements, and you should always read the two in conjunction.

Turnover

Turnover, also known as sales or revenues, comes first. Be careful when you compare the turnover for two companies, as it may have been calculated differently. For one company, a sale takes place when an order is taken or goods delivered, for another when cash changes hands.

But you can compare the company's own turnover this year and last, assuming accounting policies remain unchanged. To do this, use the figures placed side by side in the profit & loss account. If sales are up, it is a good sign, but not enough on its own to constitute a buying signal.

In the notes to the accounts, you will find a breakdown of turnover by each class of business and geographical segment. The same is available for pre-tax profits. Use these figures to find out where the company is generating most of its revenues, and how much scope there is for the trend to continue, and, if not, what can replace it.

Ratios deciphered

Price/sales ratio

A popular ratio for measuring non-profit making Internet companies is the price/sales ratio, expressed as a percentage. The lower this figure, the better. But look for profits too – either now or within a definable time span.

$$\frac{Price}{Sales} \times 100$$

Cost of sales

Next in the profit & loss account comes the cost of sales. These are fixed costs, so it is useful if they are not too high in hard times. Be wary if the cost of sales has risen a higher percentage than sales, as this will reduce the vital profit margin. We will define the profit margin shortly, in the next Ratios Deciphered box.

The cost of sales includes production overheads, raw materials, employees and product development. It also includes any changes in stock level, and depreciation, both areas with some flexibility of presentation.

Changes in stock levels – included in cost of sales – are calculated as opening stock + purchases – closing stock. In the UK, the Inland Revenue requires stock to be valued on the 'first in first out' (FIFO) basis, which assumes that oldest items of stock held by the company are used first.

In the US, stock is often valued on a 'last in first out' basis (LIFO) which in inflationary times can create a much smaller taxable profit than under FIFO. As a third alternative, stock may be valued as an average cost.

Depreciation

Depreciation is the amount by which the value of an asset is gradually reduced due to wear and tear. The annual amount is deducted from profits on the profit & loss account. There are various ways to calculate depreciation, and changing the method is a way to change the amount depreciated annually.

In the UK, companies typically use the straight-line method of depreciation. This way, a company with £10,000 to depreciate over 10 years, will depreciate £1,000 every year over the period.

If a company uses the sum-of-the-digits depreciation method, the depreciation charge is normally higher. Here, if an asset's useful working life is three years, you will add up the digits 1, 2, and 3 to make 6. You will divide the number of years left in the asset's useful working life by this figure. For example, in year 1, the depreciation is $3/6$ of asset value, and in year 2, $2/6$.

The highest depreciation appears in the reclining-balance method, which reduces the value of an asset by a fixed percentage every year.

The usage-based method of depreciation – based on how much the asset is used – is used for machinery. The annuity method takes account of the cost of capital tied up in the asset.

Sometimes a company will change its depreciation method to improve its profits figure. If so, it must reveal this in the accounts.

Gross profit and operating costs

Gross profit is sales less cost of sales. Next come operating costs, including administration, distribution, and marketing. Unlike cost of sales, operating costs can be reduced, which can be useful in hard times. They include, for instance, telephone expenses used to generate sales over the period even if the bill is not yet payable (the accruals principle in action).

Exceptional items are included here. These are defined as significant and unusual items that must be disclosed separately.

If operating expenses are growing faster than sales, this could be cause of concern. But it could be due to corporate investment that will pay off later.

Operating profit

Sales, less cost of sales and net operating costs, makes up the operating profit. This is also known as profit before interest and tax, or PBIT. On the prudence principle, profit, unlike turnover, is excluded from a long-term contract until it is reasonably certain – which is typically when 30 per cent of the contract has completed.

Other

Next comes the profit or loss (over book value) on any sales of fixed assets, and net interest payable, followed by profit before tax.

The tax charge

On UK accounts, the tax charge is typically less than the pre-tax profit multiplied by the tax rate. It includes corporation tax and deferred taxation.

Corporation tax

Corporation tax is paid on the company's income and capital gains, usually nine months after the company's year end. At the time of writing the rate is 30 per cent, or 20 per cent for smaller companies with taxable profits of up to £300,000, with marginal relief for companies with profits between £300,000 and £1.5m.

Note that dividends received from UK companies are not subject to corporation tax as they had been paid from after-tax profits. They are called franked income. Also, if a group pays tax overseas, it need not do so again in the UK. This is based on the so-called double taxation relief principle.

Deferred taxation

The company provides for deferred taxation on the profit & loss account only 'to the extent that a liability or asset will crystallize.' This can be a matter of opinion, enabling the accounts to be presented in an over-flattering light.

Deferred taxation adjusts the tax charge to reflect timing differences. These arise when items are charged to the profit & loss account in a different period for tax than for accounting purposes.

Timing differences arise, for instance, from the distinction between depreciation and capital allowances. Depreciation varies between companies. For this reason the Inland Revenue ignores it for tax purposes. Instead the Inland Revenue gives companies a capital allowance. This is a standard tax allowance which allows plant and machinery to be written down at the rate of 25 per cent a year on a reducing balance basis.

There are also permanent differences between the charge to the profit & loss account and the tax charge. For example, entertainment costs are not allowed for tax purposes. Past losses can be carried forward indefinitely to offset future tax. Losses can be carried back for one year.

If you compare a company from one country with one from another, note the following difference in accounting for deferred taxation. In the UK, the liability method is used. This uses the tax rate that the company estimates will be paid or recovered when timing differences reverse. Outside the UK, companies may use the deferral method, which uses the current tax rate.

Net profit

After tax, the profit & loss account shows the net profit, which is attributable to shareholders. It will often distribute part of this as a dividend.

Dividend

The final (not interim) dividend needs shareholder approval at the annual general meeting, and will be shown in the profit & loss account. The balance sheet will show a current liability representing the unpaid amount.

The company will retain the rest of the net profit to grow the business, keeping it in the profit & loss account in the balance sheet.

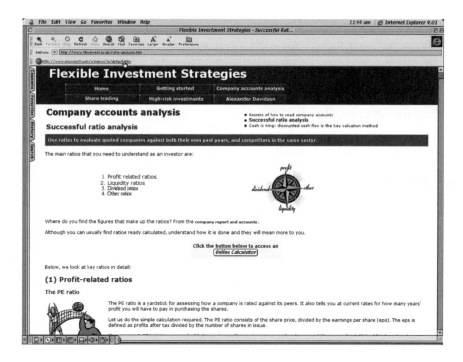

Figure 3.1 The magic of numbers

This is a reserve and is not to be confused with the eponymous financial statement.

Ratios deciphered

Profit margin

The profit margin is the net (or gross) profit, divided by turnover and expressed as a percentage.

$$\frac{\text{Net profit}}{\text{Turnover}} \times 100$$

How to use the profit margin

Compare the current year's profit margin with that of past years in the same company, or of other companies in the sector. Between different industries, margins often vary too much to make comparisons valid. They are much higher, for instance, for biotech companies than for food retailers.

Ratios deciphered

Earnings per share

The earnings per share is profits after tax, divided by the number of shares in issue.

$$\frac{\text{Profits after tax}}{\text{Number of shares in issue}}$$

Secrets of the earnings per share

As a rule, the City likes an earnings per share that rises steadily year by year. Institutional investors are more ready to buy shares in companies that achieve this than in those that do not.

Unfortunately, this means that their accountants will use every trick available to make the earnings per share rise on a continual basis. It helps them that the earnings per share can be calculated in various ways, including on a net basis, which is standard, or on a maximum distribution basis, which assumes that all earnings are distributed as dividends. Another alternative is on a nil distribution basis, which shows what earnings would have been without a dividend paid.

If earnings are calculated on a fully diluted basis, this assumes that all share options (giving an opportunity to buy shares) are exercised. The financial press often uses the headline earnings, which exclude any profits or losses from the sale or termination of an operation, or from the sale or permanent diminution of fixed assets. In comparing the earnings per share of one company with that of another, make sure that you are comparing like with like.

Ratios deciphered

The PE ratio

The PE ratio is the share price divided by earnings per share. The higher the PE ratio, the more highly regarded the shares are. A very low PE ratio indicates a bargain share, or one that is lowly rated for a very good reason.

$$\frac{\text{Share price}}{\text{Earnings per share}}$$

The PEG ratio

The PEG ratio was popularized in the UK by private client investment guru Jim Slater and the UK Web site of the Motley Fool. It is a valuation tool for small growth companies only.

The PEG ratio is defined as the company's PE ratio divided by the average annual growth rate of its earnings per share.

$$\frac{\text{PE ratio}}{\text{Average annual growth rate of earnings per share.}}$$

If the PEG ratio is less than one, this could represent good value. But the figure is not reliable because earnings per share can be manipulated as well as calculated in various ways.

How to use the PE ratio effectively

Sometimes, the PE ratio is based on last year's earnings, and sometimes on forecast earnings (known as a forward PE). Each will usually result in a different figure. In comparing the PE ratio of companies within a given sector, make sure that you are comparing like with like.

It is not usually viable to compare PE ratios of companies in different sectors as the norm in each case can vary significantly.

The balance sheet

The balance sheet is a snapshot on a given day of how the business has used its money. Companies can choose the day for this.

The key rule of the balance sheet is that a company's assets equal its liabilities. In this way, the balance sheet balances.

In many countries, the balance sheet includes assets on one side, and liabilities on the other. In the UK, assets are on the top half of the balance sheet, and liabilities below. Here is a typical layout.

UK balance sheet

Fixed assets	
Intangible assets	x
Tangible assets	x
Investments	x
Total fixed assets	x
Current assets	
Stocks	x
Debtors	x
Investments	x
Cash	x
Total current assets	x
Current liabilities	
Creditors (short term)	(x)
Net current assets	x
Total assets less current liabilities	x
Creditors (over one year)	(x)
Provisions	(x)
Net assets	x
Capital and reserves	
Issued share capital	x
Share premium account	x
Revaluation reserve	x
Profit & loss account	x
Shareholders' funds	x
Minority interests	x
Total capital employed	x

Net assets are the same as capital employed, reflecting how the top of the balance sheet is balanced by the bottom half. On the top half are the company's assets, which are what it has, and its liabilities, which are what it owes. We will look at each in turn.

Assets

First come fixed assets, which the company is, by definition, not buying or selling as part of its business. In reality, they may be worth something different than is on the balance sheet. If you are looking for growth companies, avoid companies that spend a lot on fixed assets for small profit returns. Generally, check that a company is replacing worn out fixed assets – if so, capital expenditure should be much greater than depreciation. Machinery is often worth less than on the balance sheet.

Intangible fixed assets include such items as brand names, patents, licences, development costs, and purchased goodwill (sometimes arising if the company has bought another). Such goodwill is the difference between what the acquirer paid for a company and its net asset value.

Intangible assets are sometimes amortized – similar to depreciated – over their economic life, which is up to 20 years (extendable if the assets retain value). Brands are not amortized, partly because they have an indefinite life. It is difficult to compare the accounts of companies that have brands as the brand valuations are subjective.

Next come current assets, which, by definition, can be converted into cash within a year. These are cash or cash equivalents, debtors and stock. The most reliable is cash. Debtors can refuse to pay. Stock can lose value and, if it is substantial, indicates that goods may not be selling unless it is to meet a specific order.

If stock (or another current asset) falls in value, this will hit the profit & loss account. For this reason, some companies – particularly property developers – transfer items from current to fixed assets. Conveniently, fixed assets are valued at historical cost less depreciation and do not show any fall in value.

Ratios deciphered

Stock turn ratio

You can check how many times a year a company is converting its stock into sales through the stock/turn ratio. Simply divide turnover (or cost of sales) by stock.

$$\frac{\text{Turnover}}{\text{Stock}}$$

Ideally, this figure will become larger over the years, suggesting that the company is finding it easier to sell stock.

Debtors ratio

Check the number of days that it takes the company to collect money from its customers. Divide trade debtors by turnover, and multiply the result by 365.

$$\frac{\text{Trade debtors}}{\text{Turnover}} \times 365$$

If this figure goes up over the years, the company is taking longer to collect its money. This is not a good sign, although it need not always matter if sales are also rising.

Note factoring arrangements

Check in the notes to the accounts for details of any factoring. This is when the company sells invoices to a factoring operation in return for about 80 per cent of income collected. The factoring operation will then chase the debts and retain the proceeds for itself. Note if the factoring operation has 'recourse', which is the right to repayment from the company if the customer fails to pay its debt.

Liabilities

Current liabilities come first under this heading in the balance sheet. Included here are accrued expenses, such as salaries that have been earned but not yet paid.

Also among current liabilities is a bank overdraft, which costs a company less than the money it can make from using the cash so borrowed. But check that the company is not borrowing too much. To do this, use the gearing ratio, as described in the box below.

Trade creditors, or suppliers, are another current liability. The more of these there are, the better, because they enable the company to use cash free of interest charges. To assess the number of creditor days, use the trade creditors ratio as described below.

Ratios deciphered

Gearing ratio

The company's gearing – or borrowing level – is interest-bearing loans plus preference share capital, divided by ordinary shareholders' funds, with the total expressed as a percentage. Get concerned if this is over 50 per cent without a good reason.

$$\frac{\text{Interest-bearing loans} + \text{preference share capital}}{\text{Ordinary shareholders' funds}} \times 100$$

Trade creditors ratio

To find out how many days the company is taking to pay its trade creditors, divide the number of trade creditors by turnover, and multiply the total by 365. If creditor days are high and/or increasing, this is a good sign.

$$\frac{\text{Number of trade creditors}}{\text{Turnover}} \times 365$$

Net current assets
Current assets deducted from current liabilities makes net current assets, which are known as working capital. This is what you have available to pay bills now.

If an event is uncertain and the amount that is payable is hard to assess, it will be included not in the accounts, but in the notes to these, under the heading Contingent Liabilities.

Net assets

Fixed assets plus net current assets are total assets less current liabilities. We must then remove medium- and long-term debts, and provisions, which represent future costs to the company from past transactions or events. Net assets are total assets less total liabilities.

Ratios deciphered

Current ratio

How liquid is the company? Calculate its current ratio, which is current assets divided by current liabilities. This should ideally be at least 2, indicating that current assets cover current liabilities twice over.

$$\frac{\text{Current assets}}{\text{Current liabilities}}$$

Quick ratio

Stock may not be quickly convertible into cash. To take account of this, also calculate the quick ratio, which is current assets less stock/current liabilities. This should be at least 1.

$$\frac{\text{Current assets} - \text{stock}}{\text{Current liabilities}}$$

Net asset value

In property companies and investment trusts, look for a share price that is at a discount to net asset value. To find out the net asset value, divide the share price by net assets per share. You can calculate the net asset per share by dividing net assets by number of shares in issue.

$$\frac{\text{Share price}}{\text{Net assets per share}}$$

Issued share capital and reserves

Issued share capital and reserves make up shareholders' funds. These, coupled with minority interests, are equal to total capital employed, which is the total amount on the bottom half of the balance sheet. As we have seen, this is equal to net assets, which are the total amount of the top half.

The issued share capital consists only of those shares that have been issued to shareholders. The company may be able to issue more shares from its authorized share capital. The shares in issue are mostly ordinary shares. These entitle shareholders to all profits after tax and preference dividends have been paid, and to vote at annual general meetings.

Also among shares in issue are preference shares, which carry a fixed rate of dividend. If the directors decide not to pay this dividend, preference shareholders have no legal redress, but no dividend can be paid on any other shares in the meantime.

Share capital occasionally includes non-voting shares, which have limited or no voting rights, and warrants, which are tradable securities giving holders the opportunity to buy new shares at a set price from the company (see Week 7).

Reserves, like share capital, are part of shareholders' funds. They represent retained profit. The profit & loss account (not to be confused with the key financial statement of the same name) is the only reserve which is distributable. The other reserves, being non-distributable, cannot be used to pay dividends. However, they can be used, for instance, in scrip issues, which are a distribution of extra shares to shareholders in which the overall value of their holding remains theoretically the same as the share price is proportionately reduced to compensate.

Other non-distributable reserves include the share premium account, which contains the premium to nominal value at which shares have been issued. Others are the revaluation reserve, which contains unrealized profits, and the capital revaluation reserve, which reflects changes in the valuation of fixed assets.

How capital employed is made up

When minority interests (the proportion of a subsidiary owned by others than the parent company) are deducted from shareholders' funds, the result is total capital employed.

Ratios deciphered

Return on capital employed

The return on capital employed (ROCE) is a standard measure of management performance. This is profits before interest and tax (PBIT), divided by year-end assets less liabilities, and expressed as a percentage. Ideally, the ROCE will be steadily rising over the years, and higher than for rival companies.

$$\frac{\text{Profits before interest and tax}}{\text{Assets less liabilities}}$$

The way forward

In this section, we have covered an enormous amount of ground. Do not expect to have taken everything in at first reading. Many investment professionals spend their lives analysing financial statements and still have a lot to learn.

Try this short quiz on what you have learnt before. For each question, choose only one of the three answers. Check out your score. Then go straight on to Week 4, where we will continue to unravel the mysteries of the company report and accounts.

Investor power quiz

1. The profit & loss account includes:
    (a) Profits and sales.
    (b) Assets and liabilities only.
    (c) The impact of inflation on at least the last 10 years' results.

2. Net profit is:
    (c) Profit after administrative expenses but before tax.
    (a) Profit after tax.
    (b) Profit of fishing companies.

3. Earnings per share is:
   (b) Profit before tax, divided by the number of shares in issue.
   (a) Profit after tax, divided by the number of shares in issue.
   (c) Neither of the above.

4. Net current assets are:
   (a) Short-term assets less short-term liabilities.
   (b) The reputation of the company's staff.
   (c) Quantity of buns cooked by a bakery in the financial year.

5. Prudence requires the company to:
   (b) Employ at least 10 per cent of its staff on short-term contracts.
   (c) Switch auditors at least every two years.
   (a) Take probable losses into the profit & loss account, but not potential gains.

6. Liabilities on the balance sheet are:
   (a) What the company owes.
   (b) What is owed to the company.
   (c) Members of staff who do not justify their salaries.

7. The chairman's statement is:
   (c) A statement of profits and losses.
   (a) A means of promoting the company, but which may contain some truths.
   (b) A signing off indicating whether the accounts are fit and proper.

8. The PE ratio is:
   (a) The share price divided by earnings per share.
   (b) How much your stockbroker works out in the gym.
   (c) Your personal equity compared with your age.

9. Which of the following is an asset on the balance sheet:
   (c) Creditors.
   (b) Earnings per share.
   (a) Machinery.

10. UK listed companies publish annual accounts:
    (a) Every year, with interim accounts after six months.
    (b) Every month.
    (c) When they wish.

Answers

The only correct answers are (a).
Give yourself one mark for every (a) that you answered and no marks
for (b) or (c). Now check the list below to see how you scored:

8–10. Congratulations. You have a grip on the basics of accounting
so far.

5–7. You have a fair knowledge of accounting so far, but there are
some gaps in your knowledge.

0–4. It will be helpful for you to reread this chapter.

More **secrets of the financial statements**

Your flexi-program

This week is the sequel to Week 3. By the time you have finished both of these sections, you should have an excellent broad knowledge of how to interpret a company report and accounts.

We will first look at the all important cash-flow statement, and the importance of hard cash to a company. Next comes the auditor's report and the statement of recognized gains and losses. We will delve into group accounts and the secrets of creative accounting. We will look at the impact of inflation on accounts, and international accounting.

Financial statements

The cash-flow statement

The cash-flow statement is arguably the most important part of the accounts as it shows only cash movements. Unlike profits, these cannot be fudged. Here is what a cash-flow statement looks like.

A basic cash-flow statement
£,000

(1) Cash flow from operating activities	x
(2) Return on investment and servicing of finance	(x)
(3) Taxation	(x)
(4) Capital expenditure and financial investment	(x)
(5) Acquisitions & disposals	(x)
(6) Equity dividends paid	(x)
	(x)
(7) Management of liquid resources	x
(8) Financing:	
Proceeds of share issue	x
Reduction in debt	(x)
Increase in cash for the period	x

Let us now review each section.

(1) Cash flow from operating activities
The statement may present cash flow from operating activities in a direct way as cash received from customers, less cash paid to suppliers, employees and others.

More usually, the statement will present the same figure in an indirect, more complicated way, and will reconcile the operating profit to the operating cash flow. It starts with the operating profit, and adds back depreciation, as this is not a cash flow. Any increase in debtors is subtracted as it means less cash for the company while the debts are outstanding. Any decrease in stocks or increase in creditors is added back, as it means more cash.

Preferably, net cash from operating activities on the cash-flow statement will be roughly the same as or – better still – higher than the operating profit on the profit & loss account. If it is much lower, there has been creative accounting at work. In addition, cash flow per share divided by earnings per share is a useful ratio. If this is more than 1, it indicates value.

(2) Return on investments and servicing of finance
This includes cash inflows and outflows related to payment of interest, and non-equity dividends.

(3) Taxation
Here is the cash actually paid in the year for tax (typically not the same as the tax figure on the profit & loss account), and any rebates from the tax authorities.

(4) Capital expenditure and financial investment
Here are cash inflows and outflows arising from buying and selling of fixed assets (typically vehicles or heavy machinery).

(5) Acquisitions and disposals
This contains cash movements from the acquisition or sale of any subsidiary, associate or joint venture.

(6) Equity dividends paid
This records cash flow from the payment of dividends to equity shareholders.

(7) Management of liquid resources
Here the cash flow related to the company's current investments is shown. These must be easily convertible to cash at around the value shown on the financial statements.

(8) Financing
Cash flows related to receipts from or payments to external money lenders are shown here. The company may borrow money or issue shares. It can also buy back shares, or redeem bonds.

Conclusion
The total of the cash flows represents the increase or decrease in cash for the year. In the notes to the financial statements, cash movements will be reconciled to net debt. If the reconciliation is positive, it will show a net funds figure.

How analysts focus on cash flow

Analysts also look for healthy free cash flow. Although definitions vary, free cash flow is basically the operating profit, with depreciation added back, and adjusted for various cash flows including changes in working capital, taxation, and buying and selling of fixed assets.

Discounted cash-flow analysis

As a favoured stock valuation technique, analysts generally look at the present value of the underlying company's future cash flows. They calculate the cash flows over the next few years, including a terminal value, and discount these back to a present day value by applying a discount rate on a reverse compound basis. The resulting present day value, like any projection, is not reliable. There are too many uncertain variables, including the discount rate applied, and the time period of the future cash flows. But because so-called discounted cash-flow analysis focuses on hard cash rather than easily manipulated earnings, it has a high degree of credibility.

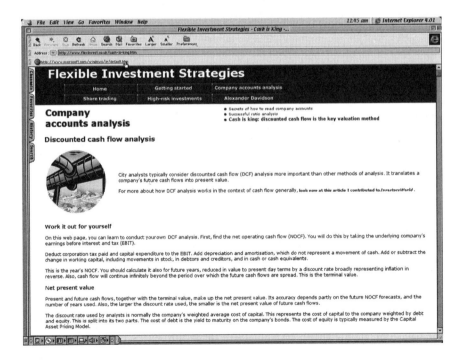

Figure 4.1 Discounted cash flow analysis

Ratios deciphered

Cash flow/earnings

Check a company's cash flow in relation to earnings. Divide cash flow per share by earnings per share. If the result is more than 1, you have probably found value. If it is much less, creative accounting has probably been at work.

$$\frac{\text{Cash flow per share}}{\text{Earnings per share}}$$

EV/EBITDA

Capital-intensive companies, such as in the telecoms industry, may have no profits, rendering the earnings per share useless. In such sectors, many analysts prefer to use the EV/EBITDA ratio. This is enterprise value or EV (market capitalization plus debt less cash), divided by earnings before interest, tax, depreciation and amortization (EBITDA).

$$\frac{\text{Enterprise value}}{\text{EBITDA}}$$

This cash-flow related measure ignores interest payments for these companies' typically huge borrowings, and so arguably presents a realistic valuation. It also has limitations, and is currently out of fashion.

Statement of recognized gains and losses

The statement of recognized gains and losses links the profit & loss account (ie the financial statement) to the balance sheet. It shows any profit or loss, regardless of whether it is included on the profit & loss account.

Here, any revaluation of fixed assets, and the effects of any relevant currency movements, are set out clearly.

The auditor's report

The auditor's report is required except for very small companies. It must say if the accounts have been properly prepared, and that required information was made available, with satisfactory explanations where required. It must confirm that the audit was properly conducted.

It must say if the accounts show a true and fair view. To achieve this, they must contain information 'sufficient in quantity and quality to satisfy the reasonable expectations of the readers to whom they are addressed,' according to the Accounting Standards Board.

The auditor is not supposed to detect fraud, but must indicate uncertainties that seem important for understanding the accounts. The auditor may issue a qualified report in the absence of information confirming that proper accounting records have been kept, or in the case of disagreement about facts disclosed in the accounts.

In a qualified audit report, the auditor can say the accounts do not give a true and fair view. Less damaging, but still serious, is when the auditor says that it cannot form an opinion that the accounts are true and fair.

If a company has a qualified audit report, do not risk investing in it. If you have done so already, sell immediately.

Group accounting

If a company has more than 50 per cent of shares in another, the latter is a subsidiary. The group prepares consolidated accounts, which combine the subsidiary's accounts with its own, as well as, separately, accounts for the parent company. Subsidiaries are a fixed asset in the parent's, but not the group's consolidated, balance sheet.

If a company owns less than 20 per cent of shares in another company, this is an investment. If a company owns more than 20 per cent but less than 50 per cent of shares in another company, this is known as a participating interest unless there is evidence against this.

If the participating interest, as is usual, also exercises a significant influence on the operating and financial activities of the other, the latter is an associate.

A joint venture has been defined as 'an entity in which the reporting entity holds an interest in a long-term basis and is jointly controlled by the reporting entity and one or more other ventures'.

The equity method of accounting

Associates (and joint ventures) are represented in a company's accounts using equity accounting. This way, the group includes in one line in the accounts only its own share of the associate's net assets. Goodwill from acquiring the asset is included with its value (rather than with any other goodwill). Every year the value of the company's share of the net assets is adjusted for value. The consolidated cash-flow statement includes dividends received from associates separately.

In the past companies have used the equity method of accounting to represent their accounts in a more flattering way. In the 1980s, the associate sometimes took out a loan that the group was liable for. Conveniently, the group would not show the amount under borrowing or interest in its accounts. It would instead be revealed under loans from associates. Under the heading Contingent Liabilities, it would be noted that the company had guaranteed the debt of an associate.

The gross equity method of accounting

The gross equity method of accounting, similar to equity accounting but more detailed, is used for joint ventures. Here, the balance sheet shows the company's share of gross assets and liabilities as well as net investment. The profit & loss account shows its share of turnover, profit, interest and tax.

Creative accounting

Creative accounting was prominent in the 1980s. Since then, accounting standards have tightened up substantially. For example, acquisitive companies can no longer exploit goodwill to show a profit on asset sales instead of a loss. This is because the accounting treatment of goodwill has changed.

But some areas of creative accounting still thrive, although I would not go quite as far as accountant and journalist Ian Griffiths who, in his famous primer *Accounting for Growth*, said that every set of published accounts is based on books which have been gently cooked or completely roasted.

Development costs

For example, development costs are conventionally charged to the profit & loss account immediately. But some companies capitalize them on the balance sheet as a fixed asset. To receive this accounting treatment, the development must be for a clearly defined, and ultimately profitable, project that the company has the resources to complete.

Under this treatment, the costs of development are amortized, hitting the profit & loss account gradually over the period expected to benefit. All research – as opposed to development – cannot be capitalized and must be charged immediately to the profit & loss account.

If you are considering investing in companies that capitalize development costs, be suspicious. In the past, some companies have done so to artificially enhance their profits on projects which are later written down in value. Query whether any development asset in the balance sheet could be sold for what it is represented as being worth, should the company run into trouble.

Capitalizing interest

If a company borrows money to build a property, for instance, it may capitalize the interest payments. This way, it again need not write off the interest immediately as a charge to the profit & loss account, and so profits for the year are increased.

This practice is widely accepted as interest is a genuine cost of a property development project. Also, the interest expense is, this way, matched more closely with income than if it hits the profit & loss account in one go before the project starts. This accords with the accruals accounting principle.

The problem is that opportunities for capitalizing interest when stock markets are doing well can encourage a company to spend beyond its means. Companies have sometimes bought other companies for debt, capitalizing the interest on the debt. Sometimes, it turns out that they cannot repay it.

Ratios deciphered

Interest cover

Interest cover, which is operating profit divided by net interest (including capitalized interest) payable, tells you if the company can finance its net interest out of current profits.

$$\frac{\text{Operating profit}}{\text{Net interest payable}}$$

Check in the notes to the accounts how much interest, if any, has been capitalized. Capitalization of interest or of development often starts and stops at different times for different companies, making fair comparisons difficult.

Accounting for leases

Now let's take a brief look at accounting for leases. The lessor owns the asset, but passes the risks and rewards of ownership to the lessee in return for rentals. From the lessor's perspective, the finance lease is accounted for as a loan, and the amounts due from the lessee as a debtor.

From the perspective of the company leasing the asset, if it has the benefits and risks associated with owning it, the asset must be included on the balance sheet whether or not it is legally owned by the company. This is according to the accounting principle of substance over form.

This rule applies, for instance, to any asset bought under an HP agreement, even though the company does not own it until it has paid off all the instalments. It also applies to any assets leased on a long-term lease (known as finance lease). By definition, in a finance lease, the present value of lease payments should be at least 90 per cent of the fair value of the leased asset. The assets capitalized on the balance sheet will be depreciated over their life, which is the shorter of the lease term and their anticipated useful life. The lease rentals will be divided between interest and capital. Interest is charged to the profit & loss account, while capital repayments reduce a total for the leasing company that is included under Creditors on the balance sheet.

Operating leases, which are short-term leases, do not provide the benefits of ownership and are not assets on the balance sheet. Instead, they are off-balance-sheet financing, which is conveniently inconspicuous in accounting terms. Their lease rentals are charged to the profit & loss account as an operating cost.

The distinction between finance and operating leases is not always clear. Some finance houses have presented finance leases that technically qualify as operating leases.

Exchange rates

The exchange rate, and how the exchange differences are accounted for, can have a direct impact on reported profits. For profit & loss account transactions, the exchange rate used is as at the transaction date, or (if fluctuations have not been too great) the year-average rate. On the balance sheet, monetary items are valued at the year-end closing rate, with exchange gains and losses taken onto the profit & loss account.

Companies sometimes borrow in a foreign currency to cover their investment in a foreign subsidiary. Subsequently, any change in exchange rates will affect both assets and liabilities on the balance sheet, so creating a neutralizing effect.

Some companies practise currency mismatching, also known as interest rate arbitrage. They borrow money in currencies where interest rates are low, and invest it in currencies where interest rates are high – in the hope of making a quick buck. This can be profitable in the short term, but is risky in the long term. A company may gain on the interest differential but lose on currency exchange rate losses.

Pension schemes

A company and its employees will often contribute to a pension fund invested on their behalf. In the past, this has proved a risk, as when the late Robert Maxwell stole from the pension fund of his firm.

Such an event will not easily happen again as rules have tightened up and a company pension scheme's funds are now under the control of independent trustees. The pension can exist in one of two forms.

First, the pension may be defined contribution. In this case, how much employees receive on their pension will depend on investment performance.

Second, and more usually, the pension will be final salary (or defined benefit). Here, employees will receive a proportion of their final salary on retirement. When calculating contributions, the actuaries involved must estimate wage inflation.

A pension holiday arises when the company does not contribute to the pension fund for a while as there is enough cash in it to meet obligations. The fund's surplus arises from greater investment returns, or lower wage increases, than anticipated.

Inflation

Alternatives to historical cost accounting

In preparing financial statements, UK companies use historical cost accounting based on the costs that the company has incurred in the year. In the profit & loss account, revenues and costs relate to sales made at the time. On the balance sheet, assets are shown at the lower of cost or net realizable value.

This approach provides an inaccurate picture of a company's financial performance because it fails to take account of inflation. Accountants have duly devised ways to account for inflation.

Current purchasing power, for instance, restates items in the financial statements with an adjustment for changes in the Retail Price Index. In the event, this may not represent the company's specific experience, so the adjusted accounts may not present a true and fair view as required. In the UK, it is only the utilities sector that uses this method of accounting regularly.

A more accurate alternative is current cost inflation, which is based on the specific price inflation experienced by the company. If there are increased year-end costs, this includes a cost of sales adjustment, and a monetary working capital adjustment based on extra investment in credit needed. Extra depreciation, based on revalued assets, will be included. As a result, the company is likely to show reduced profits.

International accounting

Outside Western Europe and the US, accounts can be opaque. An independent body known as the International Accounting Standards

(IAS) Committee aims to standardize accounting principles in major world countries. At the time of writing it has 119 members in 88 countries.

The accounts are not everything

The accounts tell you about a company's past, and give you some clues as to what may develop. But for the future there are many variables, so the accounts are not everything. It helps to talk to analysts, and to representatives of the company itself.

Investor power quiz

Answer each the following 10 questions, ticking only one of the three possible answers. Then check your score.

1. The cash-flow statement gives you:
    (a) Analysts' estimates of how much cash the company ideally needs.
    (b) Details of cash coming in and out of the company.
    (c) Details of directors' personal cash positions.

2. The statement of recognized gains and losses:
    (b) Links the profit & loss account to the balance sheet.
    (a) Links the cash-flow statement to bank statements.
    (c) Neither of the above.

3. If the auditor's report is qualified, this means:
    (c) The accounts definitely show a true and fair view.
    (b) There is disagreement about facts disclosed in the accounts, or not enough information to see if proper accounting records have been kept.
    (a) The auditors who produced the report have all passed the relevant accounting examinations.

4. If a company has a subsidiary:
    (a) This is not included in the accounts at all.

(c) This is a participating interest, and is therefore represented using equity accounting.
(b) This is included as a fixed asset in the parent's balance sheet.

5. To capitalize expenses on the balance sheet instead of charging them to the profit & loss account:
   (a) Is not allowed under any circumstances.
   (b) Is unconventional but sometimes legal.
   (c) Is compulsory under accounting legislation and the norm for companies.

6. A quoted company that has acquired an asset under an HP agreement:
   (a) Must cancel the agreement. HP agreements are not allowed any more due to accounting complications.
   (c) Need not include it ever in the company report and accounts.
   (b) Must include it on the balance sheet, even though it does not own it.

7. The exchange rate, and how exchange differences are accounted for:
   (a) Are irrelevant to reported profits.
   (c) Are kept entirely secret, so it is unknown what impact they have had on reported profits.
   (b) Can have a direct and observable impact on reported profits.

8. Operating leases are:
   (c) Assets on the balance sheet.
   (b) Off-balance-sheet financing.
   (a) No different from finance leases, and the accounting treatment is in every case the same.

9. A pension holiday is when:
   (a) The pension fund managers go on vacation and any buying and selling on behalf of the fund stops.
   (b) The company does not contribute to the pension fund for a while as there is enough cash in it to meet obligations.
   (c) Contributors to a pension fund are given a free holiday abroad as an occasional bonus. This applies only if the fund has outperformed dramatically.

10. In preparing financial statements, UK companies use:
   (b) Historical cost accounting in most cases.
   (a) Accounting that always takes inflation into account.
   (c) Neither of the above.

Answers

The correct answer is (b) in every case. Give yourself one mark for every correct answer. Now check the list below to see how you scored:

7–10. You have a good grasp of how areas of interpreting financial statements covered in this section work.

5–6. You have a fair understanding of this section, but could benefit from reading this chapter again.

1–4. You don't yet have a good knowledge of this section, but no matter. Reread this chapter.

How to make a killing on new issues

Your flexi-program

In recent years, many private investors have got their fingers burnt investing in new issues. This is because they don't understand the rules of the game. If you are to play to win, you have to be streetwise, and sometimes to have a trader's mentality. By the time that you have finished Week 5, you will understand how this market works, and will be equipped with the vital tools to make money on new issues.

First steps

How new issues work

A new issue of shares takes place when a company is floated on the stock market. This is a process that takes place over several weeks after much preliminary preparation. The banks involved must promote the deal to institutions and sometimes to private investors, which involves setting the right price, and intense promotional activity, culminating in taking orders. This is known as building a book, a process that we will examine in detail in this section.

Secondary placings

Once the company has floated, it can launch a secondary share placing. This is a way to raise further cash, and it can be done over several weeks, or in just one day. Alternatively, it may launch a placing and open offer, in which shares are placed with institutional investors. These shares placed are subject to clawback in an open offer by existing shareholders, who, under terms of the offer, will have the right to receive a set number of shares in proportion to those that they already own.

Rights issues

If the company is raising more than 10 per cent of its existing market capitalization (share price × number of shares in issue), it is obliged to launch a rights issue. In this process, which is quite time-consuming and expensive, existing shareholders are offered rights to further shares in proportion to their holding.

If, for instance, there is a 1 for 3 rights issue, shareholders will have the right to buy one new share for every three they already hold. The new shares are cheaper than the existing shares. For this reason, after the rights issue has taken place, the share price evens out to a level slightly below that of your original shares.

If as a shareholder, you are offered the chance to participate in a rights issue, do so only if you are happy with how the company plans to use the cash. If so, this is a way of picking up new shares without paying a stockbroker's commission. If you decide not to get involved, you can sell your rights in the market for cash.

Your opportunities

Many share placings are exclusively for institutions, or almost so. But as a private investor, you can get involved in some. In a bull market, you can make a killing on new issues.

In such cases you can buy into a new issue at the start, or after it has started trading and the share price has settled down, and sell out at a handsome profit. But you need to be very careful about your timing.

If the new issue is hot, the sector or prospects may not matter if you buy and sell quickly. This is known as flipping, or stagging, the stock. The professionals do it as a matter of course, and so sometimes should you.

If, however, you are buying a not so hot stock, perhaps in less than optimum market conditions, or if you plan on holding it for longer than a couple of weeks or so, you should be much more selective. You need to invest in a winning stock, at a fair valuation.

These criteria are harder to assess in a new issue than in a quoted company, due to the lack of available information.

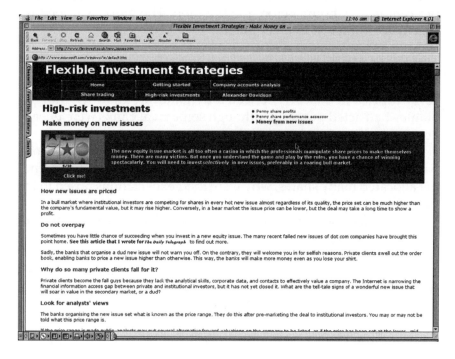

Figure 5.1 New issues

The right sector

Get the sector right and you can make your fortune. Get it wrong and you can lose your shirt. This is what happened when I invested in lastminute.com, a consumer products provider, at the height of the craze for Internet stocks in March 2000. Although I have been described as a seasoned and expert investor, I have made my mistakes and this, unfortunately, was one of them. As I wrote in the *Daily Telegraph* at the time, I played in the casino that is the stock market and lost.

I will explain to you how and why this happened as it is a lot more constructive than detailing my successes. At the time, lastminute.com had only losses, but City professionals were saying that Internet companies did not need profits. The company had a 1999 turnover of less than £200,000 but the experts said that it was future revenues that counted, an eventual profit driver.

In this case, the US investment bank Morgan Stanley was organizing the deal, and it raised the share price range – the perimeters within which the new issue price would be set – by a staggering 67 per cent just 48 hours before the flotation. The move whipped up speculators' interest to fever pitch.

Not quite Nirvana
As the share issue was ultimately 40 times oversubscribed, the revised price had clearly reflected demand. In this way, Morgan Stanley had acted properly, although some rival banks were uneasy about the way it had handled the pricing.

'The lastminute.com deal was particularly badly managed,' one banker told me. 'If it was known that private investors would not get allocated many shares, why were their expectations raised in the first place?'

To raise the price range of a new issue of shares sharply ahead of its pricing is not uncommon in a bull market. Retail investors are often then allocated only a small amount of shares – in the case of lastminute.com just 35 shares costing £133. This is claimed to protect them from the consequences of their greed. Perhaps so, but it also excludes them from potential pickings.

Even then, in the case of lastminute.com, we investors could have made a profit if we had been able to sell on the first day of trading, offloading shares we had bought for 380p for a high of 555p at one point, less dealing costs. But this was impossible as we had not been issued the share certificates required for dealing.

lastminute.com sent us an e-mail notification that these certificates would be sent out on Tuesday, 22 March. The company claimed that they would be sent first class, which should have meant arrival the following day. When, by Thursday, my share certificates had not arrived, I decided to complain. After being kept waiting on the line to the company's head office – with a promotional spiel being blasted into my ear – I was eventually given the number for a 'help line'. It turned out to be a dud, and I was offered a 'definitely live' replacement line which was in reality an answer phone message. The company's e-mail facility for urgent queries took days to yield an unhelpful reply, the delay attributed to a queue of thousands of enquirers. It was only when I started making threats that my enquiry was addressed – by the share registrar and not by lastminute.com.

The hardest hit of the Internet sectors

lastminute.com was in the business-to-consumer (B2C) sector of Internet technology. This was the worst hit by the downturn in Internet stocks that started in late March 2000. The sector has to date not recovered. Too many companies had been unsuccessful imitating the B2C model of Amazon, an online bookseller that has seen significant fluctuations in its own share price.

It was safer to invest in the business-to-business (B2B) sector, but this had its share of losers. Few Internet service providers or portals did well, partly because they were operating on a business model that found it hard to make profits. The quoted Internet companies that survived, including lastminute.com, are now typically trading at a fraction of their previous share price. At the time of writing, it is almost impossible for young Internet companies to launch new issues (also known as IPOs – international public offerings).

The pendulum will swing, and some Internet and high-tech companies will come to the market. How do I know? Because I keep a professional eye on what the venture capitalists (VCs) are up to. From the companies that they are backing now will be selected the future IPO candidates.

Even if a good VC is backing the company, this does not mean that you will make money from its flotation. The deal will be timed to give the VC an exit from its investment early at a handsome profit. The priority is never to provide a good investment opportunity for you.

How a flotation works

Where is best to float?

Most companies that look to float in London would prefer, if practicable, a full listing on The London Stock Exchange. The Alternative

Investment Market (AIM) has the appeal of fewer rules, which particularly benefits small companies that plan to make acquisitions. The OFEX – an off-exchange market where much smaller companies are traded – is the poor relation, but can offer a springboard to a full or AIM listing, and a trading facility for its shares. For more about AIM and OFEX, see Week 7.

To compete with world markets, the Exchange has been relaxing some of its rules for this. For example, the three-year trading record required for a full listing no longer applies to all high-tech companies.

The beauty parade

If you are investing in new issues, the price that you pay for your shares can be crucial. If you pay too much, you may never see a profit. It is the bank or broker organizing the entire deal – known as global coordinator and bookrunner – which sets the price, based on feedback from investors during a pre-marketing phase.

This is a prestigious job with high fees. Usually, banks will compete for the role of bookrunner in what is known as a beauty parade. The company launching the new issue (IPO) will select from a number of highly qualified candidates. What are the criteria?

Mike Lynch, the chairman of Autonomy, an Internet software company, told me that when he was appointing banks to his various secondary share offerings, he looked for an understanding of his complicated business by the banks' research teams. Clearly some high-tech analysts are more clued up than others. Another deciding factor was whether the bank has strong facilities for distributing shares in the US where Autonomy's competitors were strong.

The level of fees charged can vary, and is not usually the most important factor. In a large issue of shares, two banks are typically appointed as joint bookrunners and global coordinators, and it is important that they are able to work well together. The recent track records of the candidate banks are scrutinized.

Banks may be unable to take on the role of bookrunner if there is a perceived conflict of interest. If a bank is launching an IPO of one betting company, to take a recent example, it cannot simultaneously do the same for a rival in the sector.

If a candidate bank has an existing relationship with the company, it may be particularly well placed to launch the new issue. In the UK, the vast majority of recent new issues and secondary placings have been handled by banks that have a corporate relationship with the company.

The beauty parades are supposed to be secret. But those in the industry know which banks are pitching for which business, and the names of the winners are usually leaked in the press before they are formally confirmed.

The global coordinators, once appointed, may be in no hurry to launch an IPO or secondary placing. They are likely to hang back if market conditions are poor as, in such a case, they will find it difficult to sell the deal to institutions at anything like a reasonable price.

Getting a syndicate together

The global coordinator will appoint a syndicate of banks to help place stock with institutions and private clients, and will announce an overall fee structure.

In the syndicate, there may be one local bank that typically handles private clients (known as retail). Every bank in the syndicate is given a prestigious title such as co-lead manager or co-manager.

Pre-marketing

Pre-marketing enables banks to assess demand for a deal. In this phase, the global coordinators will meet with clients, and present the investment case for the company that they are bringing to market. From these meetings, they will get a pretty clear idea of how the company should be priced.

Based on feedback, they will set a preliminary price range. As we saw in the example of lastminute.com, this represents the proposed perimeters within which the new issue will later be priced. The analysts working for the banks in question duly produce supportive valuations on the IPO candidate.

The banks will often, but not always, make their price range public. If they do, pay close attention to this range, and to any comment on it that you read in the press, particularly if it quotes analysts from banks uninvolved in the deal. Such analysts are likely to be quite critical. Keep an eye on the Lex column in the *Financial Times*, where useful comment on new issues sometimes appears. Another useful service for this purpose is Citywire.co.uk (www.citywire.co.uk).

Occasionally, the global coordinators move the price range up or down. This means that the bank did not anticipate the level of demand for the shares correctly. If the shift is downwards, do not be surprised if the banks postpone the deal.

The bookbuild

Next comes the bookbuild, when the banks actually sell the deal to institutional investors. With large clients, they establish one-to-one meetings in which they present IPO candidates. In addition, they hold group presentations. There is typically also some video-conferencing.

All this is known as the road show, which takes place often across Western Europe and the United States. Parties presenting to institutions will include the IPO candidate's chief executive officer, its finance director, and its head of corporate communications. On the banks' part, relevant corporate financiers and analysts will partake.

Bookbuilding is a tense time for the banks handling the pending new issue. Sometimes they find it difficult to assess progress as orders don't start coming in until the end. The biggest risk is that adverse news impacts the company. This can destroy interest that institutions had initially showed. The flip side is that good news can stimulate further interest.

A traditional bookbuild lasts perhaps two to three weeks, or longer in difficult market conditions. This takes much of the time of the key individuals running the company. The longer the bookbuild, the more time there is for something to go wrong – or right.

The accelerated bookbuild

Partly because of the disadvantages of a bookbuild lasting three or more weeks, banks have instead opted for what is known as the accelerated bookbuild. This way, the bookrunner will take a company's shares on to its books, typically on behalf of an institution selling a huge stake, and will offer them instantly to its client institutional investors. It will sell the shares typically within a single day – allowing two days in case this should be needed. Occasionally, an accelerated bookbuild will take longer, perhaps three to five days.

The role of the media

Media support for the deal helps to sustain interest. If the *Financial Times* and other newspapers suggest that there is poor interest in taking up shares and that the IPO candidate is a dud, this will influence institutional investors adversely.

The financial PR agencies try to manage newsflow in order to minimize or prevent such bad press. They set an agenda and many journalists are prone to follow it. The few maverick journalists who won't play ball produce the valuable output for the private investor, flawed as their articles often are.

Pricing the deal

The global coordinators advise setting the price as high as the market will stand. The issuing company usually agrees to this. The deal gives the company a chance to raise new money but also for existing shareholders to sell out.

The deal will often be priced so that it is technically oversubscribed. This can create an impression of demand for the shares. In reality, this demand may have been so weak that it forced the share price down.

With private clients partaking in a deal, banks can set the price higher. This is because private clients are more loathe to sell out in the aftermarket than institutions. They will keep the price buoyant.

If the deal looks as if it will be priced highly, do not buy at issue. Instead, wait until the shares are trading in the secondary market. The share price may by then have fallen, creating a genuine buying opportunity for you.

How to apply for new issues

Internet brokers may offer you suitable new issues, and so may advisory brokers. Sometimes they will offer you a deal that it is hard to find elsewhere. You can also buy from one of the Web sites that specialize in new issues, although these are tending to merge or otherwise to go under. For Internet company flotations, you must typically apply directly to the issuing company, through its own Web site.

By all means invest in new issues abroad. You can sometimes do this through your normal online broker. But, remember, it can be difficult on some exchanges to keep abreast of share price movements or company-specific events.

The allocation

If you are buying via the Internet, you will download a form, which you must complete and send with your cheque to the global coordinator. Fill in the form correctly. Do not make multiple applications as these are easily discovered and can result in prosecution.

Do not expect to receive too many shares. It is the institutions that get priority as they are investing much more money than you are.

Research before you commit your money

Be wary of glowing recommendations on new issues delivered via the Internet. A company can sound very good and its technology impressive, whereas, in reality, it can be a dud. You must conduct your own research.

If you are feeling bold, try ringing the syndicate desk of the global coordinator to a new issue. This way, you may find a friendly person who will discuss the deal. But be careful as he or she will almost certainly present the deal in the best possible light and hide any problems.

Sometimes, an analyst within the firm will say a little more about the IPO stock than the syndicate desk, but this is unlikely during the sensitive period that precedes a deal. You are better off ringing up analysts at investment banks uninvolved in the deal, and asking for their opinion.

Financial journalists tend to be more objective than analysts. They will sometimes write stories based on information leaks from banks anxious to scupper the business of their rivals, or from disgruntled employees. But journalists are often surprisingly ignorant about the markets on which they focus. This means that bankers can in some cases manipulate them.

The message is clear. Take your information from a number of sources, including analysts, journalists, and, of course, the company's own Web site. Ring up the company's finance director and, if you get through, ask searching questions.

Media sources

The magazine *Investors Chronicle* is good on new issues. So is *Shares*. If you want to read about what is going on from the capital markets perspective, read *Financial News*, a weekly magazine aimed at bankers. You can register via its Web site (www.efinancialnews.com) for e-mail updates.

Also take a look at *International Financing Review*, a subscription-only magazine published by Thomson Financial, which also has a Web site (www.ifr.com). I declare an interest as I write extensively for this publication.

Do not expect objective comment from Web sites that promote new issues via the Internet. These sites are interested only in getting across their sales message. However, they will give you useful facts about the deal, including how much money is being raised, the banks involved, what the company does, how long it has been operating, and details of the management. You may find related interviews here, and a prospectus for downloading.

Grey market

By the way, check out the value that the major spread betting firms such as IG Index or City Index put on a pending new issue before it is priced. Such so-called grey market prices are a barometer of sentiment. They are not, however, based on knowledge of the book of demand for the shares, and so are an unreliable predictor. Consider grey market prices only in conjunction with your other research.

When to sell

Once you have bought into a new issue, consider flipping the shares, ie selling them quickly, once secondary market trading starts. If the shares had been overpriced at issue, this is particularly important.

The global coordinators will discourage you from selling the shares quickly. If too many investors sold out, this would send the share price plunging. The bank would then have to support the share price.

Although the bank will try to encourage private clients to hold stock, it will not dare to press institutional investors similarly as it needs them to participate in future share offerings.

Let us look at an example of this. In the July 2000 IPO of mobile telephone retailer Carphone Warehouse, bookrunner Credit Suisse First Boston gave private investors priority allocation only if they committed themselves to holding the shares for three months. It did not make a similarly restrictive proposition to institutional investors.

Investor power quiz

Now it is time to do our regular quiz. Answer each of the following 10 questions, ticking only one of the three possible answers. Then check your score.

1. To flip a new issue of shares is:
    (a) To double up on your investment.
    (b) To say nasty things about it.
    (c) To buy and sell quickly in succession.

2. The bookrunner is:
    (c) The bank or broker that organizes a new issue of shares.
    (b) A market maker in shares that were recently a new issue.
    (a) A spread betting firm that takes odds on new issues.

3. The price range is:
    (b) The target price for a new issue.
    (c) The perimeters within which the price of a new issue will be set.
    (a) The gap between the price of shares at issue, and after a month of trading in the secondary market.

4. An accelerated bookbuild is:
    (a) A collection of books that are helpful about investment. These have been acquired very quickly.
    (c) An offering of secondary shares to institutions within a short time period, typically a day.
    (b) A new issue that is promoted by at least 10 banks at once.

5. From which of the following sources can you buy a new issue?
    (a) A stockbroker, if you have been dealing with him or her for at least two years, and do not owe the firm any money.

(b) The share registrar or, sometimes, the London Stock Exchange.
(c) A stockbroker, an Internet new issues promoter, or the company itself.

6. A beauty parade is:
    (a) The girls who assist at company presentations during the road show that precedes a new issue of shares.
    (c) A number of banks competing to become the bookrunner in a new issue.
    (b) Written documentation, complete with photographs, designed to represent a flotation candidate in its best light.

7. Venture capitalists like to buy shares:
    (a) At the time of the flotation.
    (c) Well before the flotation, so that when it happens, they can exit at a handsome profit.
    (b) At least two months after the IPO, when the price has had a chance to settle down.

8. It is best to buy new issues:
    (c) In a bull market.
    (b) In a bear market.
    (a) Any time – market conditions are irrelevant.

9. Flotations on the Alternative Investment Market (AIM):
    (a) Are strictly temporary as the companies will always graduate to a full listing.
    (b) Are for the companies that have a so-called alternative (outside the mainstream) business plan.
    (c) Are for small companies, and the rules are more relaxed than for a full listing.

10. New issues are:
    (b) Most often for private investors only, although sometimes institutional investors get a bite of the cherry.
    (c) Offered as a priority to institutions. Private investors are second best in allocation.
    (a) Distributed equally between institutional and private investors, according to securities industry regulations.

Answers

The correct answer is (c) in every case. Give yourself one mark for every correct answer. Now check the list below to see how you scored:

7–10. You have an excellent knowledge of new issues – and how they work. Put it to good use.

5–6. You have a fair knowledge of new issues, but could benefit from reading this chapter again.

1–4. You haven't grasped everything in this chapter. Read it again before you invest in any new issues.

How **to win as a penny share punter**

Your flexi-program

Penny shares are an extremely exciting branch of stock market investing that are really a form of gambling. This week, you will learn what penny shares are, and how to spot the good ones, as well as when to buy and sell. By the time you have finished this section, you will be well placed to play risky but sometimes highly lucrative penny share games.

First steps

Penny share bargains

Many investors dream about making a killing out of penny shares. This is the faster, sexier end of the stock market. It is my own favourite arena. It is where you can make or lose a fortune.

In penny shares, upward momentum, usually driven by sentiment, becomes self-perpetuating, as new investors rush to buy. If you get in early enough, you have a real chance of snapping up an undiscovered bargain. This is because the mainstream City does not bother much with penny stocks, and the analysts do not find it worthwhile covering them.

Buy for growth potential

It is precisely because a penny stock is so small that it has greater growth potential than its larger counterparts. If a company has £60,000 in net profits, it could easily triple these, and, if it has a share price of 7p, this could easily double. You cannot expect the same for a company with, let us say, £2 million in net profits or a share price of 250p.

It is the opportunity for fast capital gain that makes me particularly excited about penny shares. This is partly why in my early career I specialized as a dealer in the sector. I found out then that the winners were massive but quite rare, the also-rans and losers frequent. To discover the likely winners has never been easy, and penny shares have never been for widows and orphans, but that is all part of the fun.

What is a penny share?

What is the animal that we are talking about? The essence of the penny share is that it is cheap, but there is disagreement on the price perimeters. I personally tend to think of penny shares as costing £1.00 or less. These are the criteria used by, for example, *The Penny Share Guide*, which is a major newspaper in the field. Another newsletter, *Red Hot Penny Shares*, sets the criteria as a market capitalization (share price × number of shares in issue) of £350 million or less. I also have a sneaking fondness for the tiddlers priced at under 20p or so.

The price of a penny share moves mainly on news and rumours. If the market becomes interested, the price may soar far higher than fundamentals justify. In such a case, be ready to buy and sell quickly. Should a company that is grossly overvalued on fundamentals overextend itself, investors will sell out in droves, and the share price will plummet. Eventually, stocks will find their true value, although this can take time.

A gamblers' paradise

In short, the value of penny shares can shift with the wind of investor opinion. The pennies are more fickle than larger shares. For this reason, they are more dangerous, but also more promising.

I have known a lot of dealers as well as investors in this sector. On either side of the fence, some remain in the game, but many have flunked out. Of investors, a few get rich from the pennies, but most have lost money. Of dealers, most make money, some fortunes.

Games market makers play

If you are an investor rather than a dealer, the odds are stacked against you. There is often only one main market maker in the stock, although others may follow its lead. The spread typically is wide and the dealing size small. If, for example, the bid-offer prices on a share are 9–11, this gives a spread of 2, which is 20 per cent of the mid-price of 10. In percentage terms, this is far higher than the typical spread on a large blue chip company. But penny shares can sometimes soar in value, covering and surpassing the spread within hours or even minutes.

If market conditions have been bearish, the stock could be rising from a very low base. This could be a very good time to buy, but do not become blind to the risks. I have seen investors empty their building society accounts and even take out overdrafts to punt out a favoured speculative stock. In most cases, this is madness. Always treat your investments in penny shares (or anything else, with the possible exception of aesthetic investments such as paintings, coins or stamps) as a business proposition. On the positive side, your losses will be limited as penny shares rarely go bust. As an alternative, the company may be taken over.

But penny shares can fall in value as fast as they can rise. The downside here is that it is always harder to sell than it is to buy. If you start selling in any significant quantity, the market maker is likely to create obstacles by dropping the price constantly. You may have the opportunity to deal only in limited sizes, 5,000 shares or perhaps 2,000. The next time that you deal, the price may be lower and the spread higher.

In such a way, a spread may initially appear acceptable, but it can rapidly get worse. On a spread priced at less than 10p, an additional 1p on the spread has significant impact. During a severe downturn, you may, for practical purposes, find yourself locked into your penny shares. This is all part of the game.

Become your own penny stock expert

To give yourself a realistic chance of succeeding in the penny share game, you will need many qualities. Among these are boldness tempered with prudence, deep pockets but willingness to cut losses, and a desire to understand the companies in which you invest.

This leads me to the most important quality of all. You need to operate independently and to make your own informed stock picks. In the penny share game, even more than in any other area of stockbroking, it can be fatal to rely on your stockbroker or tipster completely. Above all, don't rely on advice from the specialist penny dealers. These will usually offer you stock they have bought cheap and want to offload at a higher price. They are interested in a quick profit for themselves, not you, no matter how they might claim to want to build up a working relationship with you over a period.

In the penny share business, vested interests are at work, and unseen hands often manipulate the markets. This may happen in the UK, or abroad. In the United States, penny stocks feature prominently in the National Quotation Bureau's Pink Sheets, which offer no vetting, and no protection for consumers. Some of these stocks are OK, but I have known others turn out to be fraudulent.

In Week 2, we looked at the pump-and-dump, and how professionals manipulate the share prices of stocks that they are pushing. The penny share arena is chock-full of such games. Watch for hard-sell promotions of dud stocks, and price fluctuations based on unseen stake building or offloading. Expect that it will be easy to buy dud shares, and extremely difficult or impossible to sell them.

The penny share family

Of course, not all penny shares are duds. Here is a list of my favourite types.

Asset-rich Harry

Asset-rich Harry has – wait for it – plenty of assets. The share price is at a hefty discount to net asset value. This means that, as an investor, you are getting more assets than you pay for. On this basis at least, Asset-Rich Harry is good value for money. Given its asset backing, it is unlikely to go bust and could well become a takeover target.

Lean-and-mean Lennie

When I think of Lean-and-mean Lennie, I rub my hands with delight. This is a company that is committed to (and has a track record of) cutting costs, and creating shareholder value.

Shapely Shell

Shapely Shell is a teeny bit gorgeous, which is why she often attracts new management, who see her potential. She is a shell company, which means that she has little or no substantial business of her own. She will be priced low and has a share structure that enables newcomers – perhaps already with a substantial shareholding – to seize control.

Bombed-out Bertie

Bombed-out Bertie is a potential recovery situation. The share price has plummeted, probably to the level of a few pence. The company has not yet started to recover properly, but there are signs of change. There is perhaps a sniff of takeover interest, or a change in management. Nothing spectacular perhaps, but if you are bold enough, and are a penny share punter at heart, you may choose to step in and buy.

René Recovery

Let me introduce to you Bombed-out Bertie's sister, René Recovery. She is a recovery stock. Although she has seen better days, she is well on her way back up. She has restructured her business. I love René because, if the market favours her she can double in value or much more within a few months. René is likely to become a takeover target, in which case she can turn out to be a very profitable proposition for you, if you invested in her early enough.

High-tech Tracey

High-tech Tracey is a slightly depraved girl. Investors once thought that Tracey, with her high-tech profile, was better, stronger, and cleverer than she was. Now they have reversed their views and tend to undervalue her. If Tracey has revenues, and either profits or the promise of these within a definable period, this is a good sign. If, in her field, she is a market leader or nearly so, this is also promising.

Biotech Blossom

Biotech Blossom is a biotechnology company and she is a dangerous girl. She is researching into several products. On an industry average, only 10 per cent of these will ever become commercially viable. She spends huge sums of money on R&D, and patiently waits to hit the jackpot with one of her products. It may never happen. If Blossom starts an affair with a pharmaceutical company boyfriend, this will at least tide her over financially. In return, the backer will usually want a cut of any eventual profits.

Minnie Miner

Minnie is a mining stock. She loves to be quoted on the Alternative Investment Market where she can raise small amounts of money often. Sadly, she is often a dud.

Olga Oil and Gas

Olga is an oil and gas company and she can be expensive. She spends a fortune on operating an oil rig. Before you get involved as an investor, check out her oil production levels, and the price secured for her output.

How to buy penny shares

The first golden rule is that, when you spot the stock that you want, you move fast to buy. The price can be up 40 per cent or 50 per cent within days. Don't hang about. I have seen many lose out on fantastic gains by sitting on the sidelines, too lazy or too cautious to take the plunge.

As a second golden rule, you should create a balanced portfolio. Decide how much money you are prepared to invest in penny shares. Due to their speculative nature, and the wide spreads involved, I advise that you invest a maximum of 15 per cent of your equity portfolio in these stocks. Never invest more than you can afford to lose.

The third golden rule is that, within your penny share portfolio itself, you should spread your risk. Invest in several good penny shares rather than in one favourite, and you are less likely to be disappointed.

Many investors ignore the second and third gold rules, and put a lot of money into a favourite stock. They occasionally make a fortune. I have seen investors in Geo Interactive Media, an Internet software company, hit the jackpot.

Credit where credit's due, but such investors are gamblers. They are also operating in a bull market, and have the time to watch the market closely. They have the iron self-discipline to ride a rising share price, and to sell out before it crashes.

Buy if you can in a downturn, after penny shares have fallen more than 50 per cent. Other things being equal, select a company that is likely to be taken over. Speculation to this effect can send the share price soaring.

How to sell penny shares

As an investor in penny shares, use a stop loss, or else exert a similar discipline. My advice is that you use two stop losses: a 20 per cent one as a warning signal, and a 35 per cent one that indicates you must instantly sell. Both stop losses should trail the share price, marking the designated percentage declines from the previous night's close. You may find, in time, that different levels of stop loss work best for you. That is fine.

Choose your broker carefully

If you are looking to crack the penny share game, you may find it helpful to use a good advisory broker. Tips, advice and perspectives from an old hand can save you thousands of pounds in mistakes and lost opportunities. The problem is, most brokers specializing in penny shares are far from good.

These brokers get over-enthusiastic about the shares that they push. This is infectious. But it is you who will be parting with the money, not they. They win regardless of whether you do or not as they get their cut on every deal that you make.

In view of this, choose your broker carefully. My advice to you is to avoid any penny share dealing firm that is not a bona fide member of the London Stock Exchange. Once you really understand the penny share market, you can start buying and selling penny shares through an online broker.

This way, you will pay less commission, but you will also have to make all your own buying and selling decisions. You will be looking for shares where there is, or will be, buying interest, and which are ideally also strong on fundamentals.

Valuation secrets

How tipsters value penny shares

Penny share tipsters differ in how they value shares, and some take a more vigorous approach than others. One tipster I respect is Bruce McWilliams. He edits *Red Hot Penny Shares*, a comparative newcomer to the penny share tip sheet scene, which now holds top place in the circulation ranking.

McWilliams has credentials. As a former analyst and vice-president of Citibank, he has some notion of professional stock-picking techniques. When he picks penny stocks, he ideally likes them to be pennies, as this gives room for serious growth. He favours a share price of 25p or less. If it has slipped below 5p, McWilliams says avoid. Too low a share price is for a reason, and, as an investor, you should not let greed overcome common sense.

In McWilliams's view, penny stocks should have a market capitalization (share price × number of shares in issue) of up to £30 million and not less than £5 million. This way, they should be small enough to avoid attracting much attention from mainstream City analysts. No earnings are required, but sales growth must be more than 15 per cent per year. The sector should be in favour, or likely to become so.

Earnings and assets

Generally, I am more cautious. I like to see earnings in a penny stock, although I make exceptions when the growth story is strong and the company has realistic plans to become profitable within a defined period (as in High-tech Tracey at her best).

I like stocks that trade at a substantial discount to net asset value (as in Asset-rich Harry). If a penny share falls from favour, net assets give it a defensive backbone. They make it an attractive takeover target, or – in a worst case scenario – save it from collapse.

Relative strength

I like to see relative strength in a penny stock, based on its share price performance over the last couple of months, and the last year. If the stock has outperformed the wider index, there is on past statistics a better-than-even odds that it will continue to do so. *Red Hot Penny Shares* selects stocks for subscribers partly on relative strength.

If you buy a stock with relative strength, it is likely to have a high PE ratio relative to its sector. In this case, you will be buying a stock on its momentum, and not necessarily for its fundamental value. This approach can work well with penny shares, provided you sell out before the momentum declines.

Sound management

Regardless of fundamental valuation, a penny stock needs a trigger to set the share price moving. The turning point is often when new management moves in, and starts implementing changes. If the directors are still youngish, but have a good track record, this is a far better bet than if they are bright young Internet entrepreneurs straight out of business school.

Keep an eye on any pending management changes in favoured companies by reading the relevant trade press. You should ideally buy the shares before the underlying company's new management is properly installed or has started implementing major changes. Investing at such an early stage is risky, but the rewards can be high.

If the directors are buying shares in their own company, this is a good sign. If they are selling, try to discover the reason. If they are funding a particular expense, such as school fees, this is not necessarily suspicious. But if they are selling when the company's fortunes are declining, or are about to, this is a warning sign.

Dividends

Do not necessarily expect a dividend. Any young growth company with fire in its belly will plough earnings back into the company in order to fuel growth, rather than pay it out to shareholders as dividends. This way, if the company grows successfully, the net return to you from the capital gain on the shares should be far greater than if you had received dividends. Of course, not all companies in the penny share arena achieve their growth plans, or even have them.

The racy stocks

A warning note

If the stock market and the media love a penny stock, be wary. Grossly overvalued shares may continue to rise for a while but will always at some point crash. You can theoretically ride the wave and sell out before the share price slips, but this requires more judgement, self-discipline and, above all, time than most investors can commit.

Accounting manipulations

If you buy into racy stocks, watch for accounting manipulations. We touched on these in Week 4. In the penny share arena particularly, avoid companies with too high borrowings, and be wary if assets are capitalized on the balance sheet.

Check too if the sales are genuine, or if they are recorded in the accounts before a customer is due to pay, so artificially enhancing profits. Be cautious if the company has enhanced its profits by changing its depreciation policy or period.

All these techniques are not illegal, but they can create a false impression. The market does not always discount the deficiencies enough, until perhaps something like a profit warning occurs, and the share price takes a dramatic plunge.

Two specialist markets

Now we will take a look at two specialist markets where penny stocks are often listed. These are the off-exchange (OFEX) market, and the Alternative Investment Market (AIM).

OFEX

I admit to a little prejudice here. I love the off-exchange (OFEX) market, for all its weaknesses. This is the laxly regulated junior market which harbours some of tomorrow's stock market stars. As an investor, your task is to spot which companies have this promise, and which are more likely to sink.

You will find that there is no substitute for talking to management. If you are interested in investing in the OFEX market, I strongly recommend that you attend one of the various OFEX conferences that are held all over the UK throughout the year. You will find that OFEX companies take stalls at these conferences, and the top management, typically a bunch of idealists in their mid-thirties, will be happy to wax lyrical about their corporate hopes and dreams. JP Jenkins, the sole market maker to these companies, hosts the events with panache.

When I size up OFEX companies, I look for a business with a track record. By this, I mean a management team with experience of both its industry, and of bringing a company to market. If a blue chip company has provided backing, this is reassuring. I prefer to see some revenues and, as soon as possible, profits.

I am impressed with an OFEX company that has firm, realizable plans to make the leap to a quotation on the AIM, or a listing on the London Stock Exchange. Some succeed. But if the company simply aspires to this without having made concrete plans, be wary. The directors are well used to representing the company's prospects in the best light.

To fulfil big ambitions, an OFEX company should have clear potential for expansion. Ideally, its business will stand out from those of its competitors. Avoid stocks where a controlling family has a major stake. This makes the shares less liquid and can expose the share price to manipulation.

Do your research

For you as an investor, the OFEX market has one important advantage. It is independent of the main market. Should the FTSE 100 collapse, or soar, the OFEX will not be much affected. The companies sink or swim on their own merit.

Check out the companies thoroughly before you commit your money. Visit the official OFEX Web site (www.ofex.com) where details of individual quoted companies, complete with relevant statistics, are available free. Also, visit the Web site www.unquoted. co.uk, which provides independent news and information about OFEX.

Equities Direct (www.equities-direct.co.uk), which is a trading name of JP Jenkins, offers a dedicated service for dealing in OFEX stock. Alternatively, you can often deal in these stocks through an advisory stockbroker.

The Alternative Investment Market (AIM)

The AIM, unlike OFEX, was created and is regulated by the London Stock Exchange (www.londonstockexchange.com). Such a pedigree provides some reassurance, as does the fact that, since 1995, more than 850 companies, with a market capitalization (share price × number of shares in issue) ranging from less than £2 million to more than £100 million, have used the AIM. The market has raised more than £6.2 billion.

Never forget, however, that this is a high risk market, and shares quoted on it have proved often extremely volatile. At the beginning of March 2000, when the market for Internet companies was high, the AIM index soared to a 2,924 peak, but by May it had slipped back to 1,700, staying on that level until November 2000. Since then, the index has steadily fallen to a level that, at the time of writing, is as low as 850.

Over the period, the AIM has seen some spectacular winners, but also many equally big losers. Despite the uneven performance, the market offers considerable advantages over OFEX. The shares will usually be more liquid, and the companies more substantial. But AIM companies do not need the full 3-year track record required of most companies for a full listing on the London Stock Exchange. On the AIM, an entrant company does not have to be similarly of minimum size, with 25 per cent of its shares in public hands.

The AIM is currently benefiting from powerful promotional initiatives. In early 2002, the Exchange was making presentations in Australia and Russia about the benefits of being quoted in the AIM. The proposition was that companies might retain a local listing, but simultaneously join the AIM. In this way, they would have a dual Stock Market quotation. To pave the way, the Exchange has approved some overseas nominated advisers. Every AIM candidate must appoint and retain a nominated adviser – known as a Nomad – from an approved list.

Tax advantages

The Enterprise Investment Scheme (EIS)

Some unlisted small companies offer you, as an investor, tax relief under the Enterprise Investment Scheme (EIS). A company qualifying for EIS tax relief must be UK-based, unquoted, and carrying on a qualifying business, or intended to do so. Some industries such as financing, law, hotels, gardening and farming are barred from qualifying.

To qualify as an individual for EIS tax relief, you must be unconnected with the company in which you plan to invest. You cannot be an employee, a paid director, or a more-than-30 per cent shareholder.

If as a qualified individual, you buy shares in a qualifying company, subject to some further requirements, you can then claim 20 per cent income tax relief on an EIS investment of up to £150,000 in any tax year, and your spouse can claim the same. If you hold the shares for at least five years, there will be no capital gains tax charge on any profits. Once you have held shares for two years, your investment is exempt from inheritance tax (currently 40 per cent on the net value of an estate after £250,000 exemption).

This all sounds appealing, and it is. But never invest in a company only for its tax perks. If you lose all the money that you have invested, the tax saving will suddenly no longer seem important. Get things in perspective from the start.

Further research

Visit my Web site Flexible Investment Strategies (www.flexinvest. co.uk), where you will find the Penny Share Performance Assessor. Answer the questions online in relation to any penny stock that interests you, and my site will deliver you a firm verdict on whether you should invest or not, complete with reasons. You will also find here a wealth of information and perspectives about penny shares.

But now it's time to do our regular quiz. I have no doubt that you will really enjoy this one as penny shares are really exciting. Is your pen at the ready? Here we go.

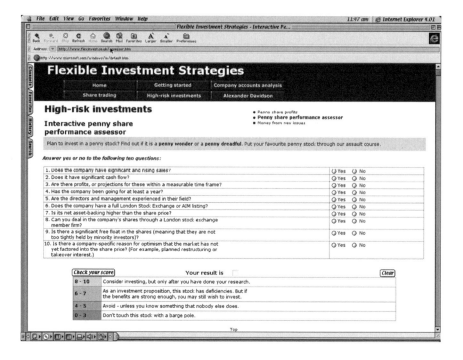

Figure 6.1 Penny share assessment test

Investor power quiz

Answer each of the following 10 questions, ticking only one of the three possible answers. Then check your score.

1. Market makers tend to give penny shares:
   (a) Wide spreads and small dealing sizes.
   (b) Narrow spreads and large dealing sizes.
   (c) The same price for buying and selling, and unlimited dealing sizes.

2. The OFEX market consists of:
   (c) Shares of 10p or less but with at least a five-year track record.
   (b) Shares of 50p or less in companies that once had a full listing.
   (a) Some young, unquoted companies that may eventually achieve a higher listing.

3. To list on the AIM, a company:
   (b) Needs a four-year track record with 20 per cent of shares in public hands.
   (c) Has to have at least three female directors on board.
   (a) Does not need a three-year track record with 25 per cent of the shares in public hands.

4. The EIS:
   (a) Gives tax relief to investors in unquoted companies.
   (c) Encourages short-term trading in enterprising young companies.
   (b) Is strictly for large, blue chip companies.

5. The AIM is regulated by:
   (a) The London Stock Exchange.
   (b) A group of private investors re-elected every year.
   (c) Nobody.

6. The definition of penny shares is:
   (c) Shares that are always with one market maker, and are priced at under 5p.
   (b) Shares which you can buy in large supermarkets and sometimes at petrol stations.
   (a) Variable, but it always refers to small companies.

7. Small companies sometimes try to make interest cover look better by:
   (a) Capitalizing expenses as assets on the balance sheet.
   (c) Giving the previous year's figure to journalists.
   (b) Nothing. There is never any attempt to make interest cover look better.

8. Penny shares have:
   (c) No accessibility for private investors. They are for institutional investors only.
   (b) No growth potential, but are very secure investments.
   (a) Bigger growth potential than large company shares, but plenty of risk.

9. The Pink Sheets are based in:
   (b) Hong Kong and (to a lesser extent) Thailand.

(a) The United States.

(c) The UK.

10. Biotechnology companies are risky partly because:

(b) They diversify too much into unrelated businesses.

(c) The people running them are often rogues.

(a) Less than 10 per cent of their products prove commercially viable.

Answers

The correct answer is (a) in every case. Give yourself one mark for every correct answer. Now check the list below to see how you scored:

7–10. You have an excellent basis of knowledge for punting on the penny share market. If you have not done so already, take a deep breath and take the plunge.

5–6. You have a fair knowledge of penny shares. Read the chapter once again, and you will be ready to take the plunge.

1–4. You haven't grasped everything in this chapter. Read it again and consider carefully whether penny shares are for you.

Make **money fast from share trading**

Your flexi-program

Trading is on a day-to-day basis more exacting than medium- to long-term investing. As a trader, you need to make money from short-term price discrepancies. It can be a nerve-racking business, and if you lose your head, you can also lose a fortune. But there is also scope to make a lot of money quickly.

You will find from this section that trading is about taking a measured risk. By the time you have finished this week, you will be equipped with all the basic knowledge that you need to get started as a trader of shares.

First steps

Become a trader

Let me start with trying to put you off, which is how the seasoned traders treat the rookies on the trading floors in the City of London. You should gain experience as a medium-term investor before you try your hand as a trader. Trading shares can be a lot more dangerous. You need access to screens that show real-time prices and relevant newsflow. Even then, however committed you are, you will be competing against professionals, and they will have advantages over you in terms of resources, backup, experience and sheer skill.

The damage can hit you hardest in a fast-falling market. In the high-tech stock meltdown from March 2000, many home-based traders lost fortunes – sometimes £70,000, £100,000, or more within weeks or days. Their main mistake? They had been tempted into retaining their losing positions in the hope of retrieving earlier gains. This almost never works. Cut your losses. The easiest way to do this is through a stop loss system (as discussed earlier in the book).

This is part of the immense self-discipline required for trading shares. Successful traders tend to be loners, stock market addicts, and committed to making money. Many stock market beginners are not suited to trading. They are attracted by the glamour of it and devastated by the reality.

Films such as *Boiler Room* and *Wall Street* make share trading seem exciting. But if you trade profitably, it can be a tedious game. It is cash gains that count, and as a trader, you can sometimes do best by skimming off small profits often, a process known as scalping. To pull this off, you will have to watch the price movements on your screen until your head starts spinning. If you see yourself as fitting into this group, read on.

Your type of trader

Decide what kind of share trader you will be. Many start with day trading. In this game, you close out your position every day. If instead you hold shares for between two and five days, you will be a swing trader. And as a position trader, you can hold shares for between one and two months.

Options and other derivatives (covered later in this section) are popular with traders. Using these, you can hedge your position in shares. There are, of course, costs involved, but this is a way to have your cake and eat it. If your core shareholding falls sharply in value, you can retrieve your losses at least to some extent by making money on related put options.

Decide on a trading plan and test it. Modify your approach as a result of trading experience into one that works for you.

Set up your office

If you are trading from home, set up a dedicated office with your telephone, PC and other screens. Have relevant financial newspapers and magazines to hand. Keep accurate records of all trading activity, including prices and dates of share purchases and sales.

You will need access to a suitable broker, and another one or two as backup. If you trade frequently, use an active trader broker. Such a firm will charge welcome low commissions, although will demand of you a minimum number of trades per month. If you trade less, a browser-based broker – the usual kind of online broker – will suit your needs. For more detail and definitions of the types of broker available, see Week 2.

From your point of view as a trader, whichever broker you end up using, do not be over-concerned about its charges. These vary, but so does quality of service, and it is this that should be your concern. I have seen traders who do perhaps 20 deals a day delight in saving a few pounds per trade on charges. For a while, this works out well. Next thing is, the broker's Web site is down and nobody is answering the phone because the skeleton staff cannot cope. This can cost you thousands of pounds or more in a single trade.

Grasp the jargon

You will quickly pick up the most basic jargon. For example, when you place your order, you must say whether it is a limit order, which specifies the price boundaries that you are willing to accept, or a market order, which is the current market price. To avoid being a victim of sharp share price movements derived from investor orders in the queue for market-makers' attention, I advise you to place limit orders. This is unnecessary only if you have access to level 11 data, which informs you of pending demand for stock, or the equivalent.

You need not bother with the more esoteric jargon. Some seasoned traders sometimes call a stock or index fluctuating within narrow bounds chop-sop, and the sixteenths which make up the spread between a given bid and ask price teenths. This does not in itself make them money.

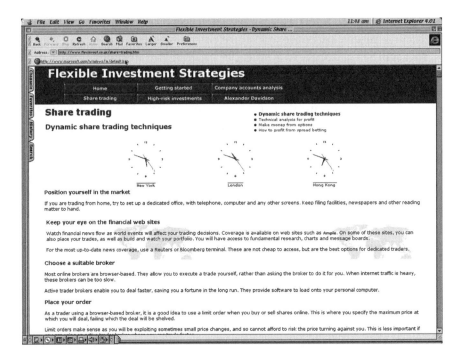

Figure 7.1 Timing is crucial for traders

Six golden rules for successful equity trading

Do not rely too much on fundamentals

In the short term, as we have seen, a stock's fundamentals will often have little influence on the share price. The main catalyst of price movement is instead investor sentiment. This is driven by company-specific or market news. Professional traders adjust their positions ahead of expected macro-economic statistics.

European markets tend to move together, usually on the back of last movements in the US market. The previous night's performance of Hong Kong's Hang Seng index will take its toll more on stocks with a strong Far Eastern presence like banks HSBC and Standard Chartered.

Some traders believe that technical analysis can help them to forecast share price and market swings. Make up your own mind about this discipline after you have completed Week 8.

Develop your own trading system and stick to it

Traders sometimes copy other people's trading systems. This rarely works for any sustained period. You need to develop a system that suits your needs. As part of this, make sure that you have access to relevant price data, analysis and charts that you decide that you need. Do not pay too much attention to Internet message boards, which are unreliable (see Week 9).

Trade only with capital you can afford to lose, and diversify your risk

As a trader, you should trade only with capital that you can afford to lose. The older you are, the less this will be. Also, do not expose more than 25 per cent of your trading capital at any given period, and make sure that this is never on just single share trade.

Buy stocks that have a reason for going up in value

If you buy a stock, it has to be because you have a good and definable reason to believe that it will rise in value. The underlying company may have just received some good news, such as that it is subject of takeover interest or has surmounted a regulatory hurdle. Alternatively, the stock may have declined too sharply in value the previous day, and be now returning to favour. The previous day's five main losers (as well as winners) are conveniently listed on some financial Web sites such as Ample (www.ample.com).

The arguments for buying are enhanced when the stock is especially liquid, which means it is easily bought and sold, in any quantity that you are likely to need, and with a reasonably narrow spread. In uncertain markets, this liquidity will not eliminate volatility in the share price, which is a requirement if you are to make money out of trading.

Sell stocks as soon as you are convinced they are losers

Cut your losses and sell stocks after they have started declining beyond a reasonable point. As we have seen, the easiest way to do this is to set a stop loss, under which, by definition, if the shares have fallen a given percentage, you sell out automatically. Charting software such as Updata's Technical Analyst can alert you when your chosen stop loss barrier is reached.

I suggest that you use a trailing stop loss (as discussed in Week 6). This way, the stop loss trails the share price. If the share price falls a

given percentage from the previous day's close, you will automatically sell out. Make the trailing stop loss 20 per cent or more, so that
if the stock fluctuates, you will not be selling out too often on a
temporary dip.

If in doubt, stay out

If you are losing money and getting despondent, pull out. In share
trading, there is always another day. Once you are out of the market,
you can analyse what went wrong. You can attempt to develop your
skills through training from experienced traders, but be careful. The
standards and credentials of trainers vary widely and are not necessarily linked to the cost of their course.

Options

The advantages of options

Options are a specialized form of investment, but they can add an
extra dimension to your opportunities if you understand how to use
the strategies properly. The key point is that they can be used either
to hedge your market condition, taking a position that is opposite
from core shares held, or for speculative trading in its own right.

Options are highly geared, and so rise and fall dramatically
compared to the underlying shares. This means you can quickly
make a large gain, or a large loss. Nick Leeson proved the point when
he brought down Barings, the investment bank, by reckless gambling
on derivatives.

Traditional and traded options

If you have a traditional option, you must exercise it (buy or sell the
underlying security) to establish a profit. Traded options, which came
to the UK in 1978, are more flexible as they can be traded, and
therefore more popular.

Traded options

You can exercise traded options, or, as is more usual, trade them in
the market. There are two types. First, a call option, which gives you

the right but not the obligation to buy the underlying security at the so-called exercise or strike price. Second, a put option, which gives you as options buyer the right but not the obligation to sell the security at the strike price. As a buyer of a call or put option, you are on the other side of the fence from its writer.

In a call option, the writer must sell the shares at the strike price if the buyer requires it. For a put option, the writer may have to buy the shares at the strike price. In compensation for taking this risk, the writer receives a premium from yourself as buyer, which is the market price that you will pay for an option. You may pay only part of the premium, otherwise known as margin, up front. If your position becomes less profitable, you will have to add cash to your margin. This is known as variation margin.

If you buy an option, you will make money if the price of the underlying share or index moves in the right direction beyond the premium you paid. The option writer will need to buy or sell shares to meet your demand. But, if the price does not move beyond the premium accordingly, the option writer will pocket the premium.

When you buy a call option, you will choose from various strike prices. If the strike price is lower than the underlying security's current market price, the option is in the money, and the difference between the strike price and the current market price is its value. If the strike price is higher than the current market price, the call option is out of the money, and the premium will be relatively low.

When you buy a put option, you also choose from a range of strike prices. If the strike price is higher than the share price, the option is in the money. If the strike price is lower than the option, it is out of the money.

As an option moves more into the money, the premium rises. As the option moves more out of the money, it becomes cheaper. When the strike price equals the current market price, the option is at the money.

How to use options

It is possible to exercise traded options, which would require owning (or acquiring) the underlying shares so that you can sell them in the market to realize your own option gain. But it's more usual – and often more profitable – to trade them, selling them in the market and so cashing in on any profit. Every buyer of an option is matched by a seller, but neither side has the odds intrinsically in its favour.

The theory sounds good, but only one in five people who play the traded options market make money. If you are going to beat the odds, you will need to be a comfortable risk-taker who is prepared to watch the market very closely. Options are a very liquid market, which means that you can usually buy or sell without difficulty.

If you are bullish

In general, if you think the underlying security or index will rise substantially and quickly, buy a call option. You may foresee this if, for example, the company is the target of a rumoured takeover bid. As a riskier alternative, you may become the writer of a put option, and will receive the premium from the buyer. Usually, the put option sold will expire worthless, and you will keep the premium without being required to buy the underlying stock. But if the share price falls below the strike price, your profits will decrease to a point when you start losing money.

As the writer of a Put option, your loss will never be more than the value of the underlying share as its value cannot fall below 0 pence. Despite this, I advise you to avoid this strategy in volatile markets. I've seen a lot of people lose money from it during sudden market corrections.

If you are bearish

If you foresee a market correction, or a downturn in an individual share, you can buy a put option. Alternatively, you can write a call option. If so, you will take the premium from the buyer and will return it if the share price fails to rise above the strike price.

If you write a 'naked' call, you will not own the shares that you are selling. If the share price collapses, you will then have to buy shares at the market price to keep your part of the deal. To avoid this eventuality, you can write 'covered' calls. This is when you sell call options on shares that you already own.

If you expect the underlying share to move significantly, but you are not sure whether it will be up or down, you can use a straddle. In a long straddle, you will buy a call option and a put option at individual strike prices and expiration dates. You will make a profit if the share price moves either up or down. But, in either case, the movement will have to be significant enough to cover the expenses of two premiums as well as the high commissions of a straddle.

When you start trading options, these are the main strategies that you need to know. As you become more experienced, you can consider more complex techniques. City professionals use puts and calls in various combinations to protect their positions as they gamble on the future direction of the stock or index.

Some techniques have colourful names such as the condor spread. The butterfly, which uses four options and three strike prices, is another favourite. There is also the tarantula, which has eight legs, each being in different futures and options contracts. These all expire on the same date.

Timing

Watch the put-call ratio. When this ratio is significantly lower than 1, buyers of call options are usually out in force. Avoid buying calls at this time as the market is likely to reverse and sellers to emerge.

Conversely, when the put-call ratio is high, there are probably many buyers of put options. At this point, avoid buying puts as buyers are likely to emerge and cause the market to rise again.

Selection

First, assess the value of the underling stock using the fundamental valuation techniques that you learnt in the sections on accounting in Weeks 3 and 4. For this purpose, you may also wish to make some use of the technical analysis techniques that are covered in Week 8. If the stock rises, call options will benefit, and, if it falls, put options will benefit. Get the stock right and your options strategy will to a large extent fall into place.

Second, check the value of the option itself, which is ultimately set by buyers and sellers. City traders use the Black-Scholes model, which sets a price for an option after taking into account its intrinsic value, time value and the fact that it does not pay dividends.

The options value will probably rise as interest rates decline. Investors will then need less incentive to use cash from deposit accounts to buy. The more volatile the underlying share price, the more chance there is of a big price move in your favour. This increases the value of the option.

Further research

If you are interested in options, read further on the subject. First visit the Web site of the Chicago Board Options Exchange (www.cboe. com). This gives you the basics readably and understandably. Do not let the US bias put you off as the principles covered are also valid in the UK. Also visit the helpful Web site www.shaeffersresearch.com. I recommend too that you obtain the Berkeley Futures free guide: *Everything you need to know about futures and options but were afraid to ask*. This is available via the company's Web site at www.bfl.co.uk.

If you are starting out as an options trader, and want to invest in small amounts, choose an options broker that is sympathetic to your needs. At the time of writing, I like Options Direct (www.mybroker. co.uk), which has less restrictions than most. Your broker should give you the price data that you need. Otherwise, LIFFE (www.liffe.co.uk) offers you 15-minute delayed prices.

Warrants

Warrants are neglected by institutions, which gives opportunities for private investors. A warrant entitles the holder to buy a specified number of new shares in a company at a specified exercise price at a given time (or within a given period). This is unlike options, which enable you to buy existing shares. Warrants are not part of a company's share capital and so have no voting rights.

Warrants tend to rise and fall in value with the underlying shares, sometimes exaggerating the movements. As with options, there is a gearing effect, with the warrants making significant moves up or down because they are much lower priced. You will pay capital gains on any profits.

If you plan to deal in warrants, find a broker that understands them. Research the market first as warrants have different conversion dates and prices. The longer the period until the warrant expires, the more likely it is that you will see a profit. But the size of the premium – how much you pay for your warrant – will reflect this.

The best newsletter about warrants for private investors is *Warrants Alert*. Find out more about this publication from the Web site www. tipsheets.co.uk.

Spread betting

The basics

Spread betting enables you to place a bet with a financial bookmaker on the direction of a share price, index, interest rates or similar. You will usually bet on futures or options. These anticipate movements in the underlying financial instrument, which means that they move earlier.

Place your bet

By way of procedure, the bookmaker will quote you a two-way price, and you will place your bet. The unit is typically £2–£5 per point on small transactions. You are betting on margin, which means you pay only 10–15 per cent of your bet up front. As a result of this gearing, you can make gains or losses quickly and of a significant size in proportion to the cash that you put up.

Before you make a profit, you must cover the spread, which is the difference between the buying and selling price. It is through the spread that the firm makes its money. If you bet on large, liquid stocks or markets, the spreads become narrower. In spread betting, you will pay no stamp duty on purchases, and – a major advantage – your profits will be free of capital gains tax.

How much capital?

Invest only with capital that you can afford to lose. Start with small bets, and become familiar through practice with how spread betting works before you branch into anything larger.

If conditions are not right, do not bet. As spread betting guru and author Charles Vintcent said recently, the usual mistake that people make in spread betting is that they bet too often.

Your peace of mind

As in other fields of investing, use a stop loss to set a limit on your losses. This may not be quite enough. Be aware that the financial instrument on whose performance instrument can fall too fast for you to apply your stop loss. You are better off using a guaranteed stop loss. The bookmaker will apply this automatically at a set level, but the spread will be wider to compensate. Note that this facility is normally unavailable on traded options.

When you are buying – as opposed to selling – it is a good idea to use a limit order. This enables you to close your bet at a predetermined profit level.

Profit from a downturn

Spread betting offers you an excellent opportunity to sell short, which involves selling an investment that you don't own with the aim of buying it back soon afterwards at a profit. Through your stockbroker, it is now difficult to sell short because settlement periods have become so much briefer than before, therefore limiting time available for manoeuvre before you settle your transactions.

Profit from price discrepancies

You can exploit differences in the spread offered by individual bookmakers. The opportunities are there, but such arbitrage is not as easy as it sounds. To make it work for you, you need to watch spreads closely and trade quickly. This takes time. Also, once you are known as an arbitrageur, the financial bookmakers are likely to close their doors to you. I have seen it happen.

Find out more

I am sometimes asked if I can recommend a course on spread betting. I tell people to avoid paying too much for this. Unfortunately, the course lecturers are all too often unable to make money from spread betting themselves, although they may claim otherwise. If you pay £1,000 or more for a day's course from a trader of dubious credentials, you are probably throwing away money.

However, journalist Angus McCrone, who really does understand spread betting, has started a day course on the subject through Global-investor (www.global-investor.com). Visit McCrone's own

Web site too at www.onewaybet.com. It has impartial information on spread betting. For my favourite book on the subject, see Week 9.

Contracts for difference (CFDs)

What is a CFD?

The CFD is a contract between two parties to exchange the difference between the opening and closing price of a contract, multiplied by the specified number of shares, as calculated at the contract's close.

Avoid CFDs until you've had experience of the stock market. They are highly risky and you will need to put up a deposit of at least £10,000 before you start trading.

How to invest in CFDs

If you invest in a CFD, you do not own the underlying share, but are entitled to dividend payments. You will need to keep your margin, which is the proportion of money you put on deposit, topped up to the extent that price movements go against you.

As an investor, you will effectively be borrowing money, and the broker will charge interest on the amount borrowed. If you go short, the broker will instead pay interest. In either case, this interest, which is slightly above base rate, is recalculated daily. You will pay no stamp duty on purchases but are liable for capital gains tax.

An opportunity for experienced traders

You can trade CFDs through financial bookmakers as well as futures brokers. They are available on the top 350 stocks in the UK, as well as on selected stocks in Continental Europe and the United States.

Speculators sometimes pick up CFDs in stocks that are expected to enter the FTSE 100 index. They buy a few days before the index entrants are announced, and sell the night before the stock enters the FTSE, from which point the share price will typically drop. For details of changes in the FTSE 100 index, visit the FTSE International Web site (www.ftse.com).

Traders also favour spread trading. Here, you buy a CFD in a likely outperforming stock, and simultaneously go short on a likely under-performer in the same sector.

Like spread betting, CFDs are a good vehicle for selling short. In April 2002, some clients of Halewood International Futures, a London broker, took the firm's advice and went short on Vodafone at 127p. The stock price fell by 15p within days after some critical press coverage. Clients made 15p a share in absolute terms, but the equivalent to 75p a share because they had put up as margin only 20 per cent of the amount invested.

More about CFDs

To find out more about CFDs, visit the Web sites of Sucden UK (www.equitycfd.co.uk), IG Index Direct (www.igshares.com) and CMC Group (www.deal4free.com).

Foreign exchange

Deal in foreign exchange

Foreign exchange (forex) trading is not investing, but it appeals to traders. This highly geared, liquid market – moved largely by macroeconomic factors – is open all day and night. There is a two-day settlement on trades.

As a trader in foreign exchange, you will buy one currency and sell another, hoping to profit from the turn. The most usual trades are between the US dollar, and either sterling or the euro. You may trade at the spot rate (cash price), which is the current exchange rate. You will pay a forward rate if you enter a forward contract to buy a currency at a pre-fixed price, at a given date.

Forex dealers and research

Many firms deal in forex on the Internet or by telephone. Try ED&F Man (www.edfman.com), Sucden (www.sucden.co.uk) and GNI (www.gni.co.uk).

Visit Trend Analysis (www.trend-analysis.com) for independent reports on currency movements.

A trading secret

If you become a successful trader, you will make mistakes. Accept this. If you are right 6 times out of 10, you will be successful. As one sales guru is fond of saying, there is no such thing as failure, only a learning experience.

Investor power quiz

How much of all this have you taken in? It is time for our quiz. Answer each of the following 10 questions, ticking only one of the three possible answers. Then add up your score.

1. A swing trader holds shares for:
    (a) One day.
    (a) Between three and six months.
    (c) Between two and five days.

2. A stop loss is when:
    (c) You sell out if the shares fall a given percentage below the original purchase price.
    (b) You take a loss only for tax purposes.
    (a) You make up losses on shares by topping up your investment with more money.

3. A call option:
    (b) Gives you the right to sell the underlying security at any price.
    (c) Gives you the right but not the obligation to buy the underlying security at the strike price.
    (a) Gives you rights to buy and sell the underlying shares at a negotiable price.

4. The writer of a call option:
    (a) Can buy or sell if he or she chooses.
    (c) Must sell the shares at the strike price if the buyer wants it.
    (b) Can always pay back the premium he or she receives, and will have no further liability.

5. A straddle is useful:
   - (a) When you expect a share not to move at all.
   - (b) When the underlying company looks as if it is about to go bankrupt.
   - (c) When you expect a share to move significantly but you are not sure in which direction.

6. A chop-sop is when a stock:
   - (b) Acquires a rival company at a bargain price.
   - (c) Fluctuates within narrow bounds.
   - (a) Doubles in value.

7. Spread betting trades are:
   - (a) Geared, with the profits fully taxable.
   - (c) Geared, with profits not subject to capital gains tax.
   - (b) Neither of the above.

8. Warrants:
   - (c) Are different from options in that they entitle you to buy new shares.
   - (b) Can be exercised only at the same time as options in the underlying stock.
   - (a) Are identical to options.

9. CFDs are:
   - (b) Low risk trading.
   - (a) Banned to private investors.
   - (c) High risk, and require from traders a deposit up front.

10. Which of the following is true about the Foreign Exchange Market:
    - (a) It closes for 10 minutes every hour to give forex dealers a break.
    - (c) It is open 24 hours a day.
    - (b) It is accessible only when the London Stock Exchange is open.

Answers

The correct answer is (c) in every case. Give yourself one mark for every correct answer. Now check the list below to see how you scored:

7–10. You have a sound knowledge of trading. This will stand you in good stead, but is no substitute for practical experience.

5–6. You have a fair knowledge of trading, but could benefit from reading this chapter again.

1–4. You haven't grasped everything in this chapter. Read it again if you intend to start trading.

Secrets of technical analysis

Your flexi-program

Technical analysis is the skill of forecasting share price and index movements on the basis of the charts. With the advance of computerized techniques, it has become very sophisticated. The debate nonetheless still rages as to whether technical analysis works or not. This week, we will examine the arguments for and against. We will look at the underlying principles, and how it all works in practice.

By the time that you have completed this section, you will be well equipped to start using the charts to assist in your investment decision-making.

First steps

The basics

Technical analysis involves analysing charts and various indicators to forecast future share price and index movements. It is often contrasted with fundamental analysis, which involves scrutinizing the report and accounts and calculating past and prospective ratios.

Practitioners of technical analysis believe that accurate market timing is in their own hands. Their art is unreliable, but it does influence markets as so many follow and act on it. For this reason, it is worth taking seriously. David Fuller, one of London's foremost technical analysts, told me that traders like himself make far more use of technical analysis than do long-term investors.

Nonetheless, sceptics about technical analysis – also broadly known as chartism – are ubiquitous. I recall a conversation with UK investment guru Jim Slater, in which we discussed technical analysis briefly, and he showed a distinct lack of enthusiasm.

US fund manager and author John Train is still more sceptical. When we discussed technical analysis on the phone, he argued that it was no more reliable reading the tea leaves. He knew of investment firms on Wall Street that had spent millions of dollars on installing technical analysis systems then had quietly shelved them as they did not work.

In Train's view, technical analysis appears an easy way out for those who cannot – or will not – tackle the difficult job of analysing and interpreting a company report and accounts. I would add that it also provides a good living for a good number of newsletter writers and lecturers.

How to plot your charts

With the right software package, the computer will plot charts for you instantly.

Some technical analysts prefer to do it by hand as this forces them to pay very careful attention. If you follow suit, draw your charts on logarithmically scaled paper, where the square size gets increasingly small as you move up the paper, or large as you move down. This shows your gains or losses on a percentage basis, which is the most realistic perspective. Avoid arithmetically scaled paper where the square size stays the same, so emphasizing absolute gains and losses.

Types of chart

Charts vary in, among other things, their level of detail. In the next few paragraphs, we will examine the main options.

Line chart

The line chart is useful for charting past term trends. It cuts out the noise of intra-day changes as its line plots only the closing mid- price of a share (or index level). This is shown on the Y axis, against time on the X axis, over any given period.

Point-and-figure chart

The point-and-figure chart cuts out still more noise of detail, focusing further on trends. Prices are plotted only when a significant change has taken place. When the share price rises by a given amount on a point-and-figure chart, an X is marked, and when it falls similarly, a 0.

If the share price switches direction from previous rises or falls, a new column will be started. Sideways trading with insignificant share price changes is ignored. On computer-generated charts, upward-pointing chevrons indicate price rises, and downward-pointing chevrons the reverse.

Bar chart

If you want maximum intra-day detail, go for a bar chart. As in a line chart, the share price is plotted against time. A bar is drawn for each

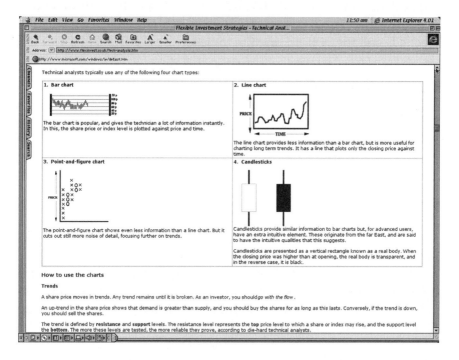

Figure 8.1 Choose your chart

day (or other time period). Usefully, each bar shows the day's high and low share prices. A tick on the left of the bar shows the opening price, and a tick on the right shows the closing price.

Candlesticks

Candlesticks originated in the Far East, and are now popular with share traders in the West. They provide similar information to bar charts but, for advanced users, include an intuitive element.

The candlestick, as it appears on the chart, is based initially on a vertical line from the high to the low of the share price. A horizontal line crosses this vertical line at the stock's opening price, and another at its closing price. The two horizontal lines are joined up on either side, creating a vertical rectangle known as a real body. If the price was lower at close than it had been at opening, the real body is black, and in the reverse case, it is white.

Equivolume charts

On an equivolume chart, price changes are correlated with volume rather than with time. The chart is in the form of a box whose width is determined by volume. The top line shows the highest price reached, and the bottom line the lowest.

Trading volumes

Trading volumes are on display at the bottom of a chart, in the form of vertical bars. Any share price or index movement revealed by the charts is more convincing if it is backed by increasing trading volume.

Chart patterns

Many technical analysts, including Fuller, have no time for the patterns which are the best known face of the craft, and notoriously unreliable. Of these, continuation patterns confirm the trend by indicating that the share price will continue in the direction that it had been taking before the pattern started. Reversal patterns indicate that the trend is changing.

Continuation patterns

The triangle

The triangle is a well known continuation pattern. It is so named because it is shaped like a triangle dwindling into a point. The zig-zag price movements represented by the triangle show a struggle between buyers and sellers. One of these parties eventually wins, and the price will break free of the triangle.

Following this breakout, the initial rise or fall of the share price is expected to correspond with the depth of the triangle. In practice, the correlation is often inexact. According to technical analysts' folklore, the more often the share price touches the side of the triangle, the more reliable is the pattern, and right angled triangles are more reliable than symmetrical.

The rectangle

Technical analysts see the rectangle as a more reliable continuation pattern than the triangle. This time, the zig-zag pattern representing

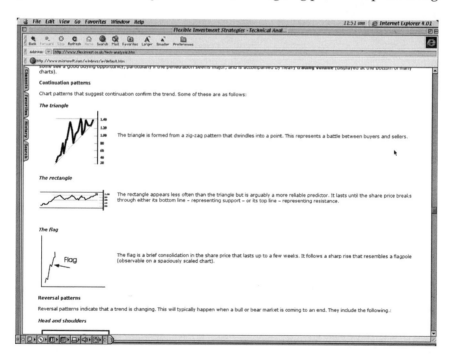

Figure 8.2 Continuation patterns

the struggle between buyers and sellers takes the form of a rectangle. A breakout can take months.

The flag

A more obscure continuation pattern is a flag. This is a brief consolidation in the share price, followed by a sharp rise like a flag pole.

Reversal patterns

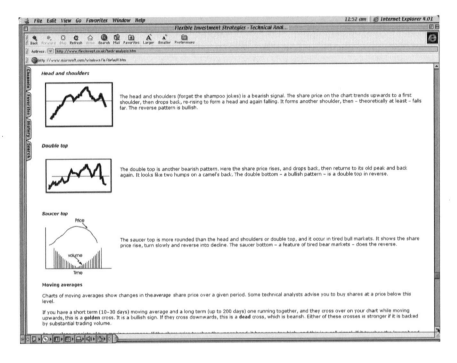

Figure 8.3 Reversal patterns

Head and shoulders

The best known reversal pattern is the head and shoulders. This is the sign of a downturn in the share price or index, as comes at the end of a bull market. In this pattern, the share price on the chart moves up and back forming a shoulder, then rises to a new high and drops back again, which creates the head. It rises to form another shoulder before dropping back to break the lowest level, which is known as the neckline.

The distance between the top of the head and the neckline is the minimum amount by which chartists expect the share price to fall below the neckline. There is also a reverse head and shoulders, with a similar measuring technique. This is a bullish reversal signal that technical analysts look for at the end of a bear market.

Double top

Another bearish reversal pattern is the double top, which is rarer than the head and shoulders. Here, the share price rises and falls in two humps, usually over at least several months. The double bottom is a double top in reverse, and is a bullish sign.

The saucer top

The saucer top, which is more rounded than the double top, sees the share price rise, turn slowly, and decline in the beginnings of a circle. It is a bearish sign. The saucer bottom is the reverse.

Beyond patterns

These patterns repeat themselves, but not reliably, and should, in my view, not be used to predict share price or index movements. That is not to say that all technical analysis does not work. US share trader and guru Marty Schwartz claims that he had got rich from using technical analysis.

In our quest to find what works in technical analysis, let's take a look at the areas on which the technical analysts agree.

Trends

The consensus is that a share price moves in trends. Once started, the trend perpetuates itself for an undefined period. The art of technical analysis is to discover a trend change early through a clearly defined reversal signal, and, if this signal is confirmed, to take action. As a technical analyst, you look only for probabilities.

Modern trend theory is rooted in Dow Theory, which resulted from the historical researches of financial journalist Charles Dow. In 1897, Dow developed two stock market indices, The Industrial Average, which consisted of 12 blue chip companies, and The Rail Average, which included 20 railroad companies. He studied these to gauge business conditions. Dow's successor, William Hamilton, developed his findings into an early version of Dow theory. This was published in 1932.

According to Dow theory, the share price reflects everything that is known about a stock. There are three trends in the stock market. In the primary trend, lasting for at least a year, a few investors buy in advance of economic recovery, and more when it actually happens. As the economy booms, there is a rush to buy, but the better informed investors are already selling.

A secondary trend, lasting one to three months, intermittently interrupts the primary trend, retracing between a third and two thirds of the gain or loss. A tertiary or minor trend lasts from one day to three weeks.

Under Dow theory, a primary trend confirmed by the two given indices will continue until its reversal is firmly signalled. A change in trend must be confirmed by more than one signal. If the share price moves up or down on the back of rising trading volume, it is likely to hold as a large number of individuals are backing the trend. If the price moves on declining volume, it may not continue as only a few buyers or sellers have set the price.

Using charts to show watch trends is fine as far as it goes. But it can be hard to detect a change in trend reliably or consistently. So how can you make money out of it?

According to the pundits, if the trend line is steadily up, you buy. If it is steadily down, you sell. The longer the trend, the more reliable it should be. When the trend breaks, you must take reverse action, buying if you were previously a seller, and vice versa.

The resistance level is the highest point to which a share or index may rise within a trend. Here, sellers move in. The support level is the lowest point to which a share or index may fall. Here, buyers move in. Once the share price has risen above the resistance level or fallen below the support level, it has penetrated the trend.

Beware of false alarms. Apparent early penetration of a trend may turn out not to be so. It is more likely to be genuine if it is substantial, backed by heavy trading volume, and instigated by important news, such as takeover interest.

The trend tunnel

A trend is more reliable if it has three tops, indicating resistance, and three bottoms, indicating support, and, in both cases, the three are in line. This way, a trend line can be drawn that touches the three tops, and a return line that touches the three bottoms. Between the trend line and the return line runs the trend tunnel.

Some technical analysts buy and sell stocks strictly within such a trend tunnel. They divide the channel in its centre by a horizontal line. When the share price is above this line, they buy, and, when it slips below it, they sell.

Technical indicators

Moving averages

The most popular technical indicators are those that show moving averages. These represent changes in the average share price over a given period. To calculate a moving average, find the sum of prices over the required number of days. Divide this by the number of prices included. If your moving average covers 10 consecutive days, this is known as a 10-day moving average. Such a short time period makes this a sensitive indicator, and so suitable for short-term investments. A 200-day moving average would prove less volatile as the averages are taken over a long period. This is more suitable for long-term investments.

Technical analysts typically keep track of two moving averages simultaneously for a chosen index or stock. A short-term moving average will indicate changes before a long-term one. Traditional technical analysis recommends that you buy shares when the price is below the moving averages, and sell when these averages start to fall. This way, it is believed that you should anticipate the market correcting itself.

The golden cross

If the two moving averages cross over on your chart as they both move upwards, this is a golden cross, which is a bullish indicator. If the two moving averages cross as they move downwards, this is a dead cross, and bearish. These signs are not wholly reliable, according to technical analysts. Like any trends, they are believed stronger if backed by substantial trading volume.

The Coppock Principle

The Coppock Principle, invented by Edward Coppock, is another indicator based on moving averages. In its original form, it shows a

10-month weighted moving average. The indicator oscillates around a zero or datum line. If it rises above this, it is a buy signal. In the 1980s, the Coppock Guide stopped working as well as it had previously. As a result, various modified versions of the original principle were invented. *Investors Chronicle* still publishes an adapted form of the monthly IC Coppock indicator for various markets.

Envelopes

Another technical indicator is the envelope, which consists of two moving averages. If the share price touches the upper band, it is a signal to sell. If it touches the lower band, it is a signal to buy.

Bollinger bands, as invented by John Bollinger, are one of the best known types of envelope. These are plotted at standard deviation (a volatility measure) levels above and below a moving average. The bands tighten when the share price is static and bulge when it is volatile. When the share price moves outside these bands, the trend is said to be likely to continue.

Overbought and oversold indicators

Overbought and oversold indicators show when the market is overbought or oversold. Stochastics is one such indicator. It is plotted as two lines that represent a share price or index in movement, one of which is a moving average of the other. These lines oscillate between 1 and 100 on a scaled chart. When either of the lines falls below 25 then rises above it, this is a buy signal. When the line overreaches 75, then slips back, this is a sell signal. If the moving average falls below the price line, this is often another sell signal.

Advanced indicators and theories

Fibonacci ratios

Some ideas in technical analysis are based on the Fibonacci ratios, invented by Italian mathematician Leonardo Fibonacci 800 years ago. Under this theory, a stock market trend is likely to retrack by 61.8 per cent, 50 per cent or 38.2 per cent.

The Fibonacci ratios inspired Ralph Nelson Elliott, a pioneering technical analyst, who published his Elliott Wave theory in 1939. In this theory, Elliott claims that market cycles have an impulse wave of five parts, reaching new highs, followed by a corrective wave of three parts. Critics of the Elliott Wave theory claim that it is not clear where one wave starts and another finishes.

Although it is controversial, the Elliott Wave theory has its fans today. Millionaire share trader Robert Beckman believes in it so strongly that he has written a book on the subject, *Supertiming*. He has said that, besides himself, there are only two others in the world who really understand Elliott Wave theory, one of whom is dead.

Gann theory

Gann theory, pioneered by master technical analyst William Gann, has its supporters and its detractors. Under Gann's quantum theory, 25 per cent, 50 per cent and 100 per cent moves in the share price are frequent, but moves of one third and two thirds less so. How far a share price moves is proportionately related to how long the move takes. Unfortunately, many starting traders are attracted to Gann as it appears to offer a simple solution to the perennial problem of timing their investments. They find out to their cost that Gann theory often does not work.

Useful Web sites and technical programs

For valuable definitions and explanations spanning technical analysis, visit the Web site of Technical Analysis from A to Z (www.equis.com/free/taaz).

To pull up specific charts, and compare the share price performance of a company with the market's, use the charting facility at FTMarket Watch (www.ftmarket-watch.com). The facility also offers moving averages. If you want to draw your own trendlines, use the AIQ charts in the mytrack program (www.mytrack.com).

If you become serious about technical analysis, investigate using a professional charting program. The Omnitrader program (www.omnitrader.com) will select the most promising investment propositions on the basis of rigorous technical criteria. Also consider the programs offered by Synergy (www.synergy.com), Updata (www.updata.com) and Indexia (www.indexia.co.uk).

A final word

I do not trust technical analysis, and advise you not to rely on it completely. Its conclusions are too often wrong. Apply fundamental analysis as well. If you ignore this advice, it is, in my view, going to cost you money.

Investor power quiz

How much do you now understand about technical analysis? Answer each of the following 10 questions, ticking only one of the three possible answers. Then work out your score.

1. Under Dow theory, how many trends are there:
   (a) One.
   (b) Three.
   (c) Two.

2. In comparison with a line chart, or a point-and-figure chart, a bar chart shows:
   (c) Less detail.
   (b) More detail.
   (a) The same level of detail.

3. Candlesticks are a form of technical analysis that originated from:
   (b) The Far East.
   (c) Scandinavia.
   (a) The United States.

4. If a favourite stock in which you have invested is continuing to rise in an uninterrupted trend, you should:
   (a) Sell the shares immediately while the going is good and reinvest elsewhere.
   (c) Continue to hold regardless of whether the trend breaks or not.
   (b) Continue to hold the shares until the trend breaks. The trend is your friend.

5. Equivolume charts work on the principle that:
   (a) At least three charts are needed to check progress on any stock.
   (b) Volume, not time, influences price changes.
   (c) The price of stocks is irrelevant.

6. Resistance is:
   (a) The bottom level to which a share price or index reaches before rising again.
   (c) The price level at which your broker personally believes that you should resist buying or selling.
   (b) The top level which a share price or index may rise before declining.

7. The triangle and rectangle are:
   (c) Reversal patterns.
   (b) Continuation patterns.
   (a) Neither of the above.

8. A golden cross is:
   (c) A mark made in yellow felt pen on a chart to indicate when you should start selling shares.
   (b) When two moving averages cross on a chart and are both moving upwards.
   (a) A lucky mascot that day traders keep beside their screens. It originated in China.

9. Bollinger bands are:
   (a) Thick elastic bands used for holding share certificates.
   (b) Two moving averages that represent the boundaries of a share's trading range.
   (c) Troupes of musical entertainers that appear at investment conferences.

10. Fibonacci ratios are:
    (b) An Italian mathematician's theory of numbers.
    (c) A form of moving average similar to the Coppock principle.
    (a) A reversal pattern favoured by German technical analysts and popular in Denmark.

Answers

The correct answer is (b) in every case. Give yourself one mark for every correct answer. Now check the list below to see how you scored:

7–10. You have an excellent knowledge of technical analysis – and how it works. But don't rely on this principle completely.

5–6. You have a fair knowledge of technical analysis, but could benefit from reading this chapter again.

1–4. You haven't grasped everything in this chapter. Read it again before you use technical analysis. Or if you don't feel convinced, ignore it and concentrate instead on fundamental analysis.

Read **and grow rich**

Your flexi-program

If you read extensively about investment, you will learn much more quickly than somebody who doesn't. It is no substitute for practice, but it is certainly a great supplement.

This week, we will look at some of the most useful reading you can do, including tip sheets, newspapers, magazines, Web sites and books. By the time you have finished Week 9, you will have lots of pointers for reading that could help you make money as a stock market investor.

Tip sheets

General

I have mixed feelings about tip sheets. The concept is sound. Tip sheets are dedicated to digging out stocks of interest to you. They will include their research in an exclusive newsletter mailed out to subscribers only. Some tip-sheet writers present a convincing case, although it is often wrong.

After reading a tip sheet, investors often buy the recommended stocks. In anticipation, the market makers often mark up their quotes, and this can send the share price soaring.

Sadly, tip-sheet writers – with only a few exceptions – lack the expertise of bona fide investment analysts. They are usually financial journalists, albeit with an interest in the stock market. Some are in it only for the money.

Aren't we all? I hear you saying. Yes, and, if the tips work out, everything in the investment garden will smell of roses. Problem is, the tips are often terrible.

One sign of a bad tip sheet is when it operates too much of a scattergun approach, ie it makes an enormous number of recommendations. The editor knows that a few of these are likely to make money for the reader, even if the rest do not. Such a tip sheet typically presents a portfolio in which the winners alone are retained, and the losers are quickly sold.

Such a buying and selling strategy conforms with a *sine qua non* of successful stock market investment, which is to cut your losses and run your profits. But in assessing its annual return, the resulting portfolio does not always take into account losses incurred on selling dud stocks acquired on the tip sheet's earlier recommendation.

There are other pitfalls. Most tip sheets encourage you to stay invested, whatever the market conditions, but this is not always giving you best advice. Being bullish sells newsletters, but it can lose subscribers money.

Most dangerously of all, some tip sheets fail to advise you to sell the losers quickly enough. As it is, private investors lose a fortune because they are afraid to cut losses. They do not want to take a small loss but sit like the proverbial toad on the aspen leaf dreaming that all will come right again although the share price is falling constantly. The tip-sheet writers that are advising them all too often make this mistake.

The flip side is that some newsletters advise you to sell the winners too early. In fact, winning stocks often carry on rising. But, in my view, the newsletters that advise a half way house – sell one half of your holding in a winning stock and keep the other – are trying to have their cake and eat it. Either the stock is worth keeping or it is not.

Tipsters under fire

Since the high-tech stock meltdown that started in March 2000 and, well into 2002, shows no real sign of recovery, tipsters have come under scrutiny. A glance at some of the more active message boards of financial Web sites reveals how unpopular some of the erstwhile gurus have now become.

Figure 9.1 Share tipsters exposed

Back in February 1999, the financial Web site Interactive Investor International (now Ample) asked its site visitors: 'Many readers think tipsters such as Tom Winnifrith, Paul Kavanagh and Michael Walters have tipped one too many duds. Do you agree?' A very high 80.39 per cent of those who voted agreed, and only 5.94 per cent disagreed. The rest did not know.

In my view, there is only one way for you to use the tip sheets to your advantage. That is as a starting point for your own research. Take responsibility for your own investment decisions, or, ultimately, in the stock market, someone, somewhere – and it could well be one of the tipsters – is going to lose you a lot of money.

My favourite tip sheets

This is the self-indulgent bit. I must admit that I am a tip-sheet addict, and subscribe to at least seven at any given time. I like to flick through a bundle of tip sheets, and note any stocks mentioned that are not on my own radar screen.

Let me tell you my favourite tip sheets. I have always loved *Red Hot Penny Shares*, which is part of the output from Fleet Street Publications, Britain's largest stock market newsletter publisher. In the subdued market conditions at the time of writing, the newsletter is recommending stocks that are cheap on fundamentals. This makes sense.

Although I am not a technical analyst, I love *Chart Prophet*, which is also published by Fleet Street. This newsletter presents a sometimes complex methodology in a simple way. If you subscribe, you will pick up the basics of technical analysis quite quickly and painlessly, a feat indeed.

The most valuable tip sheets of all, in my view, are those that apply rigorous value criteria to their stock selection. I like the publication *analyst*. Its writers describe themselves as analysts, not journalists, and their approach is heavily influenced by the stock-tipping principles of US value investor Warren Buffett. To find out more about its long-term investing approach, visit the company's Web site at www.analystinvestor.com.

Internet message boards

Access to message boards on financial Web sites is usually free, although it may have first been necessary to register with the site. These boards are great fun, both for reading and participation. At best, they can give you tips and perspectives, all of which may help to crystallize your own investment thinking. If you are investing in Baltimore Technologies, for example, it may be interesting to read the views of an IT specialist who understands encryption technology, the field in which the company operates.

At the same time, *caveat emptor* should prevail. Message boards do not, and, indeed, cannot, apply much censorship to messages that registered subscribers send, although the larger financial Web sites like Motley Fool employ someone to keep an eye on messages received and to contribute where appropriate.

The problem comes when parties use the message boards to plant recommendations that suit their purpose. If they own a stock, they may hype it up to others in the hope that this will create buying interest and send the share price soaring. If they plan to short a stock (selling shares they don't own in the hope of buying back later at a lower price), they may send messages of doom and gloom about it. Sometimes, the manipulators send persistent messages over weeks or months – using different aliases. This way, it appears that the messages derive from many sources.

How do you detect the genuine messages from the fake? Initially, you need not try. Just read the message boards and try to get a general impression. Pay the most attention to reasoned argument backed by facts. A significant number of contributors to the message boards of the Motley Fool UK Web site, for instance, have proved capable of this.

If something important is said, check the facts with the company itself on the phone. Ask to speak to the finance director or chief executive directly. You will often be referred to somebody who will help you, and you are taken more seriously if you have aimed for the top.

Newspapers

Pay attention to press coverage of the stock market, but note that its quality varies. In the case of news, it is helpful to have it immediately. Screen-based news services such as Bloomberg (www.bloomberg. com) and Citywire (www.citywire.co.uk) or Ample (www.ample. com) deliver fast. For comment, the *Financial Times* is invaluable mainly because it yields so much influence. The Lex column on the back page is widely read, although its reasoning, taken often from analysts' views, varies in quality.

In the *Daily Telegraph*, the Questor column sometimes offers an interesting commentary, and *The Times* has an equivalent in its Tempus column. Otherwise, the *Daily Mail* offers interesting gossip about companies. Its lively if superficial City pages used to be a favourite of mine, as they remain of many City workers. Also, keep an eye on the business pages of the quality Sunday newspapers, as their tips and stories tend to move markets early the following week.

When you read news, try to forecast what this means for the markets, rather than simply noting what has happened. Check macro-economic data, such as inflationary indicators. If, for instance, gross domestic product (GDP), a measure of national income, rises over 3 per cent in each of four quarters in succession, this gives a strong inflationary warning, and the Bank of England is likely to react by raising interest rates.

This adversely affects the stock market, as it makes borrowings more expensive for quoted companies. Also, many investors will leave their money on deposit for a higher return rather than using it to buy shares.

If you buy stocks based primarily on the macro-economic perspective, this is known as a top–down approach. Many top investors, including master US fund manager Peter Lynch, prefer the bottom–up approach. This requires focusing on stock fundamentals first, and the macro-economic picture only second.

Magazines

I read *Investors Chronicle*, the longest established weekly magazine for private investors. There has always been enough in it to make it worth reading, and, these days, under new editorship, it is looking really good. The magazine is crammed with facts about companies coupled with the journalist's opinion as to whether you should buy, sell or hold the shares and whether they are fairly priced or not.

When I was working at one particular major investment bank, I noticed that prominent institutional investors sometimes bought a stock partly because it was tipped in *Investors Chronicle*. This made my blood run cold as the magazine is not for professional investors, but it demonstrated how influential it is.

I find *Shares*, the recently established weekly rival to *Investors Chronicle*, enticing to read, but the quality is variable. The magazine is highly focused on trading. There is plenty on spread betting, on CFDs and traded options, on software for traders, and on technical analysis. I declare an interest as I have written for this magazine.

Courses

An investment course should be more interactive than a book, but this will normally cost you much more. It should also be regularly updated. My favourite investment course is *Secrets of Growing Rich: The Complete Investment Mastery Course*, published by Fleet Street Group.

The course impresses me because of the variety of expertise that it taps. Many experts contribute individual lessons. In the roster of writers are Peter Temple on options, Bruce McWilliams on penny shares, and many other known names. I should declare that I too have contributed lessons.

It is a truism that when many minds are working together, the power of thought created is greater than the individual parts. I am proud to be part of this course, which is kept up to date, with valuable e-mails sent out regularly to subscribers.

Other courses vary in quality. When you come across expensive seminars, always pay great attention to the reputation of the tutor. Try to find out about his or her track record from an impartial source. At the time of writing, I note that Global-Investor.com (www.global-investor.com) has launched a fantastic series of day master classes, using tutors of the calibre of Angus McCrone on spread betting and Michael Walters on small company investing.

Quality courses of this kind, although certainly not cheap, are nothing like as expensive as highly dubious seminars on spread betting and trading run by certain fly-by-night entrepreneurs.

Web sites

The Web is so large that the danger is there is too much information at your disposal. Investment (behind pornography) is one of the most popular subjects for surfers.

Do not spend too much of your time exploring Web sites that cover the more specialist areas of investment. Find one or two more general stock market investment sites that you can love, and concentrate on getting to know these. Just as with a lover, the longer you explore, the more you will understand. Pick a site that is worthy of your time and attention.

What kind of site fits the bill? I recommend one that has some or all of the following characteristics: news, analysis, investment education, interactive message boards, tips, bookshop, top five winners and bottom five losers on a daily basis, stock prices, and useful links. My personal favourites are The Motley Fool (www.fool.co.uk) and Ample (www.ample.com). In addition, I like to keep an eye on the *Financial Times* Web site (www.ft.com), which is good for news, analysis and charting.

Hemscott (www.hemscott.net) has an excellent online data base. Using this, you can input required levels, for example, on earnings per share, assets per share, dividend cover, share price, market capitalization and similar. You can then pull up a list of shares that match these criteria. For a list of other useful sites, turn to Appendix 1.

Books

You can read about books on the Internet, and order them, usually at a discount. The disadvantage to a conventional bookshop is that you don't get a book in your hand, to flick through, to feel, and to assess before you buy.

Before you buy, check the background of the author. A financial journalist may write a readable and informative investment book. That is fine, as far as it goes. Remember, however, that most financial journalists have not made much money from investing.

A better bet may be a book from an acknowledged master investor, but such an individual may not write very readably.

I like to buy books from Amazon. I love to read the online reviews provided, although they can be biased. I check the sales ratings, and which other authors buyers of the book have bought. A picture of the book cover is provided. There is a full money back policy, and the price is usually discounted. If Amazon delivered the wrong book to me, it would swiftly be replaced.

I also like Global-investor.com (www.global-investor.com), which is sometimes cheaper than Amazon. It has a superb selection of business books. There is the great advantage that you can order these easily by telephone (01703 233870) as well as by post.

Beginners' investment books

You will never have time to read all the beginners' books on the stock market, and most are, in any case, saying the same thing. The trick is to pick out the best. At the risk of blowing my own trumpet, I would recommend my own best seller *How to Win in a Volatile Stock Market* (Kogan Page, 2nd edition, 2002). In this book, I drew on my experience as a share dealer to explain how the people who invest money for a living treat their own money. Read it for perspectives that you will not find elsewhere in print.

For a lighter approach, read *Fair Shares* by Simon Rose. This book was recently revised and republished by Management Books 2000. It is an entertaining but cynical introduction to the stock market. To find out about the mechanics of share ownership, including annual general meetings, shareholders' circulars, and getting value from your broker, read *The Shareholder*, also by Simon Rose (Mercury Business Books). It is written in a deliciously irreverent style.

Also make time for *The Motley Fool UK Investment Guide*, by David Berger, a medical doctor, and his US-based mentors David and Tom Gardner (Boxtree). This is the book of the Web site. It has its faults, its biases. It is facetious and irritating. But it is also outrageously funny.

A must-read are some of the books of Jim Slater, the investment guru and former City big gun. As a share tipster, Slater has made his share of mistakes, but he has had more successes than most. For complete beginners, Slater has written *Investment Made Easy* (Orion Business) which is quite an exciting read, and less basic than it appears. But if you already know a little about investment, skip this and instead go to Slater's most famous book, his first, and, in my view, his masterpiece. This is *The Zulu Principle*, which shows you how to invest in growth companies. You will find no better guide to investment – anywhere.

For reference purposes, try *How to Read the Financial Pages* by Michael Brett (Century Business). The book is highly accessible, and is indeed recommended reading on some City courses.

If you like a chatty style of writing, do not ignore self taught investor, *Daily Mail* columnist, and TV presenter Bernice Cohen. Her first book, *The Armchair Investor* (Orion Business), aims to shatter some of the mystique surrounding stock market investment. The author is too keen on technical analysis for my liking, but she has clearly found it useful and she also covers fundamental analysis.

For an overview, read *Streetwise: Guide to beating the market and investing with confidence*, edited by Nils Pratley and Lorna Bourke (Hodder & Stoughton). Journalists who worked for the now defunct financial Web site TheStreet.co.uk put together this book. It throws light on every aspect of investing, including the new economy.

Try also some lighter books about the securities industry. I recommend *The Buck Stops Here* by Jim Parton (Simon & Schuster). This offers a hilarious description of the inner workings of an investment bank from a junior salesman's perspective. It is a terribly cynical book. It represents stockbrokers as knowing nothing, and doing boring work for extremely high pay.

Also beg, borrow or steal a copy of *Where Are the Customers' Yachts?* by Fred Schwed Jr, first published in 1940 (John Wiley). This is again a funny but cynical book about the stock market. It makes some telling points.

On high-tech stocks, the best recent book that I have read is *The Big Tech Score* by Mike Kwatinetz, with Danielle Kwatinetz Wood (John Wiley). The author is a leading Wall Street investment analyst, and has a gift for explaining his sometimes complex valuation methods and ideas simply. In addition, do not miss the timeless classic *Super Stocks*, by Kenneth Fisher (IRWIN Professional Publishing). This book shows you how to use the price/sales ratio and the price/research ratio to select bargain-basement high-tech stocks.

For a focus on the economics of markets, read *Market Movers*, by Nancy Dunnan and Jay J Pack (Warner Books). It is US-biased, but highly informative and readable. I have also found *The Economist Guide to Economic Indicators*, by Richard Stutely (Economist Books), useful. Another worthwhile read is *How to Lie With Statistics*, by Darrell Huff (Penguin), which provides insights into how statistics are manipulated.

It is worth knowing which stock market investment systems have worked better than others over a period of decades in the United States. To find out, read *What Works On Wall Street* by James O'Shaughnessy (McGraw Hill). Interestingly, a low PE ratio comes out as a strong indicator of value. One tip sheet editor I know was so impressed with this book that he has worked its theories into his stock selection procedures.

Last under this subheading, but not least, try not to miss the classic *One Up on Wall Street* by Peter Lynch (Penguin). The book – quite an easy read and written by a master US fund manager – shows how you can pick stocks using the specialist knowledge that you will have gained in your own life.

Beginners' online investing books

If you would rather invest online, read my earlier book, *Everyone's Guide to Online Stock Market Investing* (Kogan Page). In this book, I take you through everything that you need to know to get started as an online investor and to make money. I show you how to get your financial affairs in order before you start investing, how to select a suitable broker – no easy task – and how to invest using old-fashioned principles, but with the benefit of Internet technology.

I also like *Online Share Investing: A UK guide*, by Alistair Fitt, (Ftyourmoney.com). The book is good on value investing, and has a suitably cynical perspective on technical analysis. It explains how to find and use online brokers.

Trading Online by Alpesh Patel (Pearson Education) is a classic in its field. I personally find this author is too keen on technical analysis. I also find the style of writing too prosaic, and too broken up. It reads more like an instruction manual than a book, and I do not always agree with the instructions. Having said that, Patel is a successful trader and imparts valuable advice. If you read this book, you will learn from it.

You will also learn from *The New Online Investor* by Peter Temple. This is a comprehensive book, which you may wish to dip into than to read from start to finish.

There are many books that list stock market Web sites. *Stephen Eckett on Online Investing* by Stephen Eckett (Harriman House) is useful in this area. It also has excellent coverage of trading and investment techniques and on solving technical problems. The book is in fact a collection of Q & As from the author's regular column about Internet investing in *Investors Chronicle*.

Trading

For the basics of day trading, with good coverage of technical analysis, read *Understand Day Trading in a Day*, by Ian Bruce (Take That). For more sophisticated techniques, read *Market Wizards* by Jack D Schwager (HarperCollins), in which the author interviews master traders. *Stock Market Wizards* (John Wiley), a more recent book by the same author, is also worth reading.

If you can get hold of them, read the published transcripts of the Beckman lectures (Milestone Publications) in which investment guru Robert Beckman instructs on trading techniques. His style is controversial and gripping.

For perspectives on the psychology of trading, read *The Disciplined Trader: Developing winning attitudes* by Mark Douglas (New York Institute of Finance). The author advises that if you are to trade successfully, you must develop new perspectives without boundaries. Also, visit his Web site at www.markdouglas.com.

Also, don't miss *Trading For a Living*, by Dr Alexander Elder (John Wiley). This is strong on trader psychology, and technical analysis. A study guide with multiple choice questions is also available.

If it is short selling that interests you, read the classic *Evil's Good Book of Boasts* (T1ps.com). In this little masterpiece Cawky, as he is affectionately referred to on Tom Winnifrith's share-tipping Web site, explains how to sell short, and offers his personal opinions – none too high on the UK financial services industry's regulatory system.

Another wonderful opinionated read is *How to Make Your Million from the Internet*, by Jonathan Maitland (Hodder & Stoughton). The author, a well known TV broadcaster, tells the full story of how he mortgaged his house for £50,000 and tried unsuccessfully to turn this sum into £1m in a single year through day trading.

Take a cautious look at *Make a Million in Twelve Months* by James Hipwell and Anil Bhoyrul (John Blake). These two controversial former *Daily Mirror* journalists let you into their secrets of how to play the market at its own game. As their own track record showed, sometimes these techniques have worked, and sometimes not.

For an entertaining fictional perspective on trading in the City, read *Trixie Trader* (Orion), written by *Daily Telegraph* financial journalist Helen Dunne.

Incidentally, do not miss *Reminiscences of a Stock Operator*, by Edwin Lefevre (John Wiley). The book is compulsory reading for novices on some City and Wall Street trading floors. It is a fictionalized account of the life of legendary share trader Jesse Livermore and shows how as a trader you should not fight the market. Spread-betting trader and self-styled guru Vince Stanzione, among others, recommends this book to his clients.

If you want to read about spread-betting, go for *Market Speculating* by Andrew Burke (Rowton Press). It covers the pros and cons, and how to work the system to your best advantage. It has good sections on trading tactics, and on technical analysis.

If you are interested in options, read Investing in *Traded Options* by Robert Linggard (Take That). For background colour, read *Rogue Trader* by Nick Leeson (Warner Books). This is the author's own account of how he brought down Barings, the merchant bank, through reckless derivatives trading.

Technical analysis

If technical analysis is a mystery to you, I urge you to read *Charters on Charting* (Batsford). This book is oversimplified, sometimes to a ludicrous level, and occasionally patronizing, but it remains the most accessible introduction to technical analysis that has ever been written. Unfortunately, this book is out of print, but even so, try to get a copy. If you cannot, the *Investors Chronicle Guide to Charting* (FT Prentice Hall) is not a bad alternative. It is comprehensive and informative.

I also quite like Martin Pring's introduction to *Technical Analysis* (McGraw-Hill), which has a useful CD ROM with it. Once you are *au fait* with the basics, go for the same author's *Technical Analysis Explained* (McGraw-Hill). This is a psychology-orientated treatment of a subject that is all too often reduced to dull mechanical explanations.

I enjoyed – and continually go back to – *Technical Analysis of Stock Trends* by Robert D Edwards and John Magee, New York Institute of Finance). This is a seminal work, but it can be stuffy. I would not recommend that you start with it.

Finally, read the output of those who have actually made money out of technical analysis. In particular, I recommend *How to Make Money in Stocks* (McGraw-Hill), which is the masterpiece of US fund manager and guru William O'Neil. The book presents a proven stock market investing system which makes substantial use of technical analysis. Unfortunately, I recently took my copy into a restaurant in the City of London and when I briefly left my table, a pin-striped maniac picked the book up, started reading it, and walked off with it under his arm. That says it all.

Also, read Martin Zweig's *Winning on Wall Street* (Warner Books). It reveals how to use the technical indicators that Zweig, a US trader, has used so successfully.

Accounts and value investing

The best book for understanding a company report and accounts is still *Interpreting Company Reports and Accounts* by Geoffrey Holmes and Alan Sugden (Prentice Hall Woodhead-Faulkner). Buy the latest edition (7th at the time of writing).

Supplement this with *Accounting for Growth: Stripping the camouflage from company accounts* by Terry Smith (Century Business, 1996). This best seller shows how named companies have dressed up their books through creative accounting. It makes disturbing reading, although regulations have since been tightening up and some of the accounting trickery unmasked is no longer possible in the UK.

I also recommend the Interpretation of Financial Statements course that is one of the options for the Securities Institute Diploma taken by ambitious stockbrokers and investment bankers. The course is excellent, covering basic areas systematically, and involving the study of sets of up-to-date company accounts. I personally did the course through Financial Training, a London-based financial training organization which provided an excellent tutor.

For ratio analysis and related techniques, I strongly recommend *Security Analysis on Wall Street*, by Jeffrey C Hooke (John Wiley). This takes you through the modern securities analyst's armoury of valuation techniques. The specialist requirements for some individual sectors are briefly covered. For a more anecdotal approach, read *The Super Analysts*, by Andrew Leeming (John Wiley). The book contains interviews with leading players.

If you want to get to grips with the theories of Benjamin Graham, the founder of investment analysis, you could read the chapter about him in *The Money Masters* by John Train (Harper Business). More ambitiously, try Graham's own work. Start with *The Intelligent Investor* (Harper & Row), and then go on to his more complicated masterpiece *Security Analysis*.

To get to grips with the investment techniques of Warren Buffett, the billionaire investor who was heavily influenced by Benjamin Graham, read *Buffettology*, by Mary Buffett and David Clark (Pocket Books). It is the clearest book on the master's investment methods, including the annual compounding rate of return, that I have ever read. Also, dip into *Warren Buffett Speaks*, which is a compendium of quotations compiled by Janet Lowe (John Wiley).

On discounted cash flow analysis, read *The Penguin Guide to Finance* (Penguin Books) by Hugo Dixon. The author, who used to head up the Lex column in the *Financial Times*, favours back-of-the-envelope calculations over complex spreadsheet work. His book is entertaining as well as elucidating.

Dubious brokers

The securities industry is riddled with fraud. It always has been and always will be. The wide boys who used to flog shares on the phone now do so via the Internet. It is worth finding out more about how they operate in order to safeguard your money.

Read my second novel, *Stock Market Rollercoaster* (John Wiley). This will tell you the truth about how the dubious brokers work. Also, if you can get a copy, read my first book and instant best seller *The City Share Pushers* (Scope Books). This is a first hand account of how sharp share dealers have treated the public. The book was serialized by News International, and a version was broadcast on Channel 4's *Dispatches*.

Also, try *The Watchmen*, a financial thriller by Matthew Lynn (Arrow Books). The story tells of a former stockbroking analyst who becomes a fugitive after he has stumbled on an insider-dealing ring. The relationship between analysts, the press, and quoted companies comes under scrutiny.

General

For a sober warning, read *Valuing Wall Street* by Andrew Smithers and Stephen Wright (McGraw Hill, 2000). The book argues that, based on the q concept of Nobel Laureate James Tobin, today's stock markets are dangerously overvalued.

For secrets of how professional fund managers select stocks and manage portfolios, read *The City: Inside the great expectation machine* by Tony Golding (Financial Times Prentice Hall). On what motivates the City moneymen from a psychological perspective, read *Bears & Bulls: The psychology of the stock market* by David Cohen (Metro).

Investor power quiz

Answer each of the following 10 questions, ticking only one of the three possible answers. Then work out your score.

1. What are the advantages of buying investment books online?
   (a) Delivery by special courier the next day.
   (b) There is always a facility to interview the author by e-mail before you buy.
   (c) A discounted price and perhaps readers' reviews.

2. Jim Slater is:
   (c) An investment guru who writes books.
   (b) One of the largest UK business book publishers, with a US offshoot.
   (a) A UK-wide chain of investment book shops.

3. You can learn the basics of interpreting a report and accounts from:
   (a) Tip sheets.
   (c) A book or a course.
   (b) A course only. There are no good books on the subject.

4. Which one of the following is a great US fund manager:
   (a) Michael Walters.
   (c) Peter Lynch.
   (b) Bernice Cohen.

5. The purpose of reading investment books is:
   (a) To raise your general cultural level.
   (b) Entertainment.
   (c) To make more money investing on the stock market.

6. Tip sheets:
   (a) Never have any influence on share prices.
   (c) Can influence share prices dramatically.
   (b) Are always reliable in their tips.

7. Message boards on financial Web sites are:
   (a) Reliable.
   (c) Unreliable but worth watching.
   (b) To be completely ignored.

8. Is it possible to find books about the investment strategies of Warren Buffett, the great US value investor?
   (c) Yes.

(b) No.
(a) Only those written by Warren Buffett himself.

9. The Motley Fool:
    (a) Puts its name to books on the stock market for beginners.
    (b) Has a Web site.
    (c) Both of the above.

10. Writers of books on the stock market are usually:
    (a) Financial journalists.
    (b) Fund managers and investors.
    (c) Either of the above.

Answers

The correct answer is (c) in every case. Give yourself one mark for every correct answer. Now check the list below to see how you scored:

7–10. You have a good knowledge of investment reading. You are well placed to read selectively and use knowledge so gained to improve your investment knowledge.

5–6. You have a fair knowledge of investment reading.

1–4. You haven't grasped everything in this chapter. Read it again to give you a few ideas on suitable investment reading.

Time **to start investing**

First steps

Now that you have read so far, what next? The theory that you have learnt in this book is your springboard to success, but it can only take you so far. You must make your first fumbling attempts at investing.

Fantasy trading

If you do not feel ready yet to commit your money to the stock market, you could set up a fantasy portfolio. This is better than doing nothing, but it is not enough. You will not get that stomach-churning feeling which comes when you put your own money on the line. It is like learning French or German without ever speaking with the natives.

Invest for real

As soon as you can, I advise you to do some *real* investing. My advice to you is to set aside a small sum – between £5,000 and £10,000 – and to buy shares in perhaps five stocks. Do not necessarily buy the stocks all at once.

As you build your entry-level portfolio, you must watch your stocks carefully, perhaps on a week-by-week basis. It is not necessary to check stock prices daily – unless catastrophic world events, like the terrorist attacks on New York and Washington of September 11, 2001, should have an extraordinary impact.

You are investing for the medium term. Give yourself an initial six-month period. If your stocks fall below, say, 25 per cent of what you paid, sell out early using a simple stop loss system. Use the cash to reinvest elsewhere.

Keep a record of your purchases, sales, and price movements. At the end of six months, tot up whether you are in profit or in loss, taking dealing expenses into account.

Take it slowly

Don't make the mistake of becoming so obsessed with investment that you never do anything else. I say this because I know people who followed this route, but have not made money in proportion to time invested. They sacrificed relationships, hobbies, and important commitments. They now regret missed opportunities.

In the past, I have helped thousands of stock market investors find success. If you have any queries, please get in touch. Write to me via my Web site at www.flexinvest.co.uk. Alternatively e-mail me at info@flexinvest.co.uk. I look forward to hearing from you.

The lights are now fading and the show is over. I hope you enjoyed it as much as I did. I hope you get as much fun out of investing and the stock market as I do. I hope that you make some serious money, which is how you keep the score. I believe that you can.

Useful **Web sites**

Here is a list of Web sites and/or contact details that users of our Web site Flexible Investment Strategies have found useful. This is not a complete list, but it is a good starting point for your *own* researches. For convenience, it is arranged alphabetically.

Alternative Investment Market (AIM)

BDO Stoy Hayward – accountancy firm specializing in AIM
www.bdo.co.uk

Graham H Wills & Company – a stockbroker that offers IPOs in OFEX and AIM stocks
www.ghw.co.uk

Newsletter Publishing Ltd – relevant tip sheets
www.redskyresearch.com

Analysts

Consensus ratings
Hemscott
www.hemscott.net

Sharescope.com
www.sharescope.com.

Research
Analyst (detailed financial analysis for private investors)
www.analystinvestor.com

Beeson Gregory (small- and medium-sized companies in Europe)
www.beeson-gregory.co.uk

Charles Schwab (US-based analyst centre)
www.schwab.com

DLJ Direct (also access to US bureau services including Zack's
company report, and S&P MarketScope)
www.tdwaterhouse.co.uk

Equity Development (analysts' reports commissioned by companies)
www.equity-development.co.uk

Equityinvestigator (independent analysts' research on high-tech
stocks)
www.equityinvestigator.com

FirstCall Research Direct
www.firstcall.com

IDEAGlobal (former investment bank analysts' independent
research covering US markets)
www.ideaglobal.com

Institutional Investor (lists top analysts and their track record)
www.iimagazine.com

Merrill Lynch HSBC
www.mlhsbc.com

Moneyguru (own analysts)
www.moneyguru.com

Multex Investor
www.multexinvestor.com

Peel Hunt (for small subscription, research and video interviews)
www.peelhunt.com

Salomon Smith Barney
www.salomonsmithbarney.com

SG Cowen (technology-driven investment bank)
www.sgcowen.com

UBS Warburg
www.ubswarburg.com

Books

Amazon – cut-price books, and online reviews
www.amazon.co.uk

Books.co.uk – price surveys and other comparisons of online
bookshops
www.books.co.uk

Global-investor – an excellent large online bookshop
www.global-investor.com

Contracts for difference (CFDs)

How they work
Copperchip
www.copperchip.co.uk

IGIndex Direct
www.igshares.com

Sucden UK
www.equitycfd.co.uk

Some CFD dealers
Cantor Index
www.cantorindexcfd.com

City Markets
www.cityindex.co.uk

Deal4free
www.deal4free.com

GNI Touch
www.gni.co.uk

Halewood International Futures
www.hifutures.com

IFX
www.ifx.co.uk

IG Markets
www.igshares.com

ManDirect
www.mandirect.co.uk

Sucden Equities CFDs
www.equitycfd.co.uk

Complaints

The Financial Services Authority
www.fsa.gov.uk

Derivatives (options, futures and warrants)

Information/prices
Chicago Board of Traded Options Exchange
www.cboe.com

The London International Financial Futures and Options Exchange
(LIFFE)
www.liffe.com

Market Eye – derivatives exchange information included
www.thomsonfn.com

Prestel – live traded options prices
www.finexprestel.co.uk

Shaeffersresearch.com – an overview on options, and on how they work
www.shaeffersresearch.com

Warrants Alert – a newsletter on warrants, and an introductory guide
www.tipsheets.co.uk

Some options and futures dealers
Berkeley Futures
www.bfl.co.uk

Easy2Trade
www.easy2trade.com

GNI
www.gni.co.uk

Halewood International Futures
www.hifutures.com

ManDirect
www.mandirect.co.uk

Options Direct
www.mybroker.co.uk

Directors' dealings

Citywire
www.citywire.co.uk

Digitallook
www.digtallook.com

Discount brokers (financial services) – a selection

Aisa direct
www.aisa.co.uk

Alder Broker Group
www.abgltd.co.uk

Bestinvest
www.bestinvest.co.uk

Chartwell
www.chartwell-investment.co.uk

Cheapfunds.co.uk
www.cheapfunds.co.uk

Chelsea Financial Services
www.chelseafs.co.uk

Direct investor
www.direct-investor.com

Discount Investments Ltd
www.discount-investments.co.uk

Garrison Investment Analysis
www.garrison.co.uk

Hargreaves Lansdown
www.hargreaveslansdown.co.uk

Heritage Financial Services
www.heritage-financial.co.uk

Investment Discount House
www.idh.co.uk

Investment Discounts On-Line UK
www.theidol.co.uk

ISAVED
www.isaved.co.uk

Max Value
www.maxvalue.co.uk

Moneyworld-ifa
www.moneyworld-ifa.co.uk

PEP-TopTen.com
www.pep-topten.com

quickdiscounts.com
www.quickdiscounts.com

Seymour Sinclair Investments
www.seymoursinclair.co.uk

Exchanges

London Stock Exchange – a highly informative and useful Web site
www.londonstockexchange.com

NASDAQ – the US high-tech market
www.nasdaq.co.uk

Forex

News and research
Trend Analysis – an independent service offering reports on currency
movements
www.trend-analysis.com

Some forex trading firms
Cantor Fitzgerald International
www.cantor.co.uk

ED&F Man
www.edfman.com

Lind-Waldock (a US firm)
www.lindwaldock.com

Sucden
www.sucden.co.uk

Free samples (of financial newsletters)

www.financial-freebies.com

www.thefreestuffgallery.com

General

Hemmington Scott – arguably the best source of free information on UK quoted companies, including a five year summary profit & loss account with balance sheet, share price movements, major share-holders and similar
www.hemscott.com/equities/index.htm

itruffle – a lively investor resource for the small cap sector
www.itruffle.com

The Motley Fool UK – news, educational material and similar
www.fool.co.uk

High-tech stocks

Durlacher, the investment boutique
www.durlacher.co.uk/research

Richard Holway Ltd
www.holway.com

Silicon Investor
www.siliconinvestor.com

International investing

JP Morgan's ADR Web site – useful on ADRs
www.adr.com

Investment clubs

Proshare
www.proshare.org

Investment courses/educational

Basic guide to options
www.tradebasics.com

Martin Cole's four day futures trading course on the Costa del Sol
www.learningtotrade.com

Investor's Business Daily – free course online (including technical analysis) from US guru William O'Neil
www.investors.com

Sharecrazy.com
www.sharecrazy.com

The Siroc site – educational on futures and options
www.siroc.co.uk

Stock Academy – general stock market education
www.stockacademy.com

Success Investor training
www.incademy-training.com

Fantasy trading

DLJdirect – excellent demo
www.tdwaterhouse.co.uk

Hollywood Stock Exchange – fantasy trading in film stars and musicians as practice for stock market trading
www.hsx.com

Selftrade – excellent demo trading
www.europeanbrokerno1.com

Message boards

DigitalLook.com – bulletin board comments roundup
www.digitallook.com

The Motley Fool UK
www.fool.co.uk

The Motley Fool US
www.fool.com

Raging Bull
www.ragingbull.com

Silicon Investor – subscription-based but high quality
www.siliconinvestor.com

Web page providing links to message boards of Market Eye, Hemmington Scott, UK Shares and Ample (formerly Interactive Investor International)
www.freeyellow.com/members6/scottit/page7.html

Yahoo
finance.yahoo.com

New issues

Financial News – a leading publication about new issues on capital markets
www.efinancialnews.com

issues direct – a Web site specializing in new issues
www.issuesdirect.com

OFEX

Equities Direct – online broker dealing in OFEX stocks
www.equities-direct.co.uk

OFEX Web site
www.ofex.co.uk

unquoted.co.uk – news, information, interviews and message boards
on OFEX companies
www.unquoted.co.uk

Penny shares

Use these sites for background information and perspectives. If you
want to buy, I advise you to do your own research.

City Equities – UK penny share dealer
www.cityequities.com

Penny Investor.com
www.pennyinvestor.com

Penny Shares Ltd.com – an online tip sheet
www.pennysharesltd.com

Pennystockinsider.com
www.pennystockinsider.com

Penny Stocks.net – advice on US pink sheets stocks
www.penny-stocks.net

Rollercoaster Stocks
www.rollercoasterstocks.com

Research (on companies)

Corporate reports
www.corpreports.co.uk

FinancialWeb – US news, research, Securities & Exchange Commission filings, and company reports
www.financialweb.com

Hemscott.net
www.hemscott.net

Hoover's Online – online details of more than 15,000 companies worldwide
www.hoovers.com

Investor-relations
www.investor-relations.co.uk

Dr Ed Yardeni's Economics Network – US economics and stock market research from the chief global economist of Deutsche Bank Securities in New York
www.prudential.com

Zacks.com – brokers' reports and news (US site)
www.zacks.com

Search engines (our favourites)

www.excite.com
www.google.com
www.yahoo.com

Share price quotes

Teletext
www.teletext.co.uk

Spread betting

How it works
The Internet Sporting Club
www.internetsportingclub.co.uk

Onewaybet.com – our favourite Web site about spread betting
www.onewaybet.com

spreadbets.net
www.spreadbets.net

spreadbetting explained
www.spreadbettingexplained.com

Some financial bookmakers
Cantor Index
www.cantorindex.com

City Index
www.cityindex.co.uk

Financial Spreads
www.finspreads.com

IG Index
www.igindex.co.uk

Spreadex
www.spreadex.co.uk

Stockbrokers

Selection
The Association of Private Client Investment Managers and Stockbrokers – a list of brokers (online and otherwise)
www.apcims.co.uk

Money extra – online brokers compared
www.moneyextra.com

Motley Fool UK – a table comparing costs of online brokers, and
related message boards
www.fool.co.uk

Some online brokers (not a complete list)
Abbey National Sharedealing Service
Tel: (0845) 601 2201
E-mail: Nick.crabb@abbeynational.co.uk

Barclays Stockbrokers
www.barclays-stockbrokers.co.uk

James Brearley & Sons
Tel: (01253) 629400
www.jbrearley.co.uk

Cave & Sons Limited
Tel: (01604) 621421
www.caves.co.uk

Charles Schwab
Tel: (01021) 262 4497
E-mail: webinquiries@schwab-europe.com

City Deal Services
Tel: (0800) 917 8889
E-mail: shares@citydeal.co.uk

comdirect
Tel: (0870) 600 6044
E-mail: info@comdirect.co.uk

Davy Stockbrokers
Tel: 00 (353) 1679 7799
www.davy.ie

Durlacher Ltd
Tel: (020) 7459 3600
www.durlacher.com
E-mail: info@durlacher.com

e-cortal
www.e-cortal.com

egg
Tel: (0845) 1233233
www.egg.com

etrade
www.etrade.co.uk

Fastrade
Tel: (0131) 247 7399
www.fastrade.co.uk

Goy Harris Cartright
Tel: (0116) 2045500
E-mail: customerservice@ghcl.co.uk

Halifax
Tel: (0870) 2411114
E-mail: Customercare.hsdl@halifax.co.uk

Hargreaves Lansdown
Tel: (0117) 980 9800
www.hargreaveslansdownco.uk
E-mail: onlinetrading@hargreaveslansdown.co.uk

Murray Beith Murray Asset Management
Tel: (0131) 225 1200
E-mail: asset@murraybeith.co.uk

MyBroker
Tel: (020) 7903 6350
E-mail: info@mybroker.co.uk

NatWest Stockbrokers
Tel: (020) 7895 5609
www.natweststockbrokers.co.uk

Redmayne Bentley
Tel: (0113) 243 6941
E-mail: info@redmayne.co.uk

Self Trade UK Ltd
Tel: (0845) 100 0210
E-mail: info@selftrade.co.uk

The Share Centre
Tel: (0800) 800008
E-mail: info@shareco.uk

Share people
Tel: (0870) 737 8000
E-mail: info@sharepeople.com

Stock Academy
Tel: (01223) 234545
www.stockacademy.com

Stocktrade
Tel: (0131) 240 0400
E-mail: sharedealing@stocktrade.co.uk

TD Waterhouse
Tel: (0161) 819 6000
www.tdwaterhouse.co.uk

Teather & Greenwood
www.teathers.com

Torrie & Co
Tel: (0131) 225 1766

Virgin Money
www.virginmoney.com

Walker, Crips, Weddle, Beck
Tel: (020) 7253 5202
E-mail: clientservices@wcwb.co.uk

Xest
Tel: (020) 7953 2442
www.xest.com

Stock market news

Bloomberg
www.bloomberg.co.uk

DigitalLook – news alerts by e-mail on a trader's portfolio of stocks,
www.digitallook.com

Electronic Telegraph
www.telegraph.co.uk

Evening Standard online
www.thisislondon.com

The Financial Times
www.ft.com

Fleet Street Publications – Britain's largest investment newsletter
publisher
www.fleetstreetpublications.co.uk

Forbes – US business magazine
www.forbes.com

Guardian Unlimited
www.guardian.co.uk

Investors Chronicle
www.investorschronicle.co.uk

Newsletter Publishing – how to subscribe to The AIM Newsletter
(and sister publications). Sample copies provided online
www.newsletters.co.uk

News review – summary of weekend City press
www.news-review.co.uk

Red Herring magazine – high-tech developments in the United States
www.redherring.com

This Is Money – news archives of *Daily Mail, Mail on Sunday,* and
Evening Standard
www.thisismoney.co.uk

Tipsheets.co.uk – details of leading tip sheets on the market
www.tipsheets.co.uk

Tax

Blythens – tax advice
www.blythens.co.uk

Deloitte & Touche – tax advice
www.deloitte.co.uk

Details of tax rates
www.glazers.co.uk

Inland Revenue
www.inlandrevenue.gov.uk

Technical analysis

DecisionPoint.com – material on charting, some free, the rest for
subscribers only
www.decisionpoint.com

Digitallook – access to charts
www.digitallook.com

FTMarketWatch – an excellent charting facility available
www.ftmarketwatch.com

Interactive Investor International – another useful chart search
facility
www.iii.co.uk

murphymorris.com – leading market technician John Murphy
addresses subscribers
www.murphymorris.com

mytrack program – if you want to draw your own trend lines
www.mytrack.com

StockCharts.com – excellent general site on charting
www.stockcharts.com

Technical Analysis from A to Z – highly informative
www.equis.com/free/taaz

Professional charting programs

Indexia
www.indexia.co.uk

Omnitrader
www.omnitrader.com

Synergy
www.synergy.com

Updata
www.updata.com

Trading shares

Career DayTrader.com – useful articles and interviews related to day
trading
www.careerdaytrader.com

Cyberinvest – information and links for home-based traders
www.cyberinvest.com

DayTraders.com
www.daytraders.com

Robert Miner's Web site – useful advice on trading
www.dynamictraders.com

Unconventional financial advice

Eden Press – leading California-based seller of unconventional tax
haven books
www.edenpress.com

Stuart Goldsmith – seller of privacy-type information
www.stuartgoldsmith.com

The offshore secrets network – a glimpse into unconventional
offshore investing
www.offshoresecrets.com

The Sovereign Society – unconventional tax haven advice
www.sovereignsociety.com

Useful
quotations

The great investors often express the tricks of their trade simply and briefly.

You will make more money from understanding – and applying – even one or two of the following quotations (as displayed on the Flexible Investment Strategies Web site) than from a lifetime of listening to mediocre advice from many self-styled stock market pundits.

Read these quotes carefully. Think about them day and night. Put them into practice. And watch your investment performance improve.

Your judgment as an investor

'You're neither right nor wrong because other people agree with you. You're right because your facts are right and your reasoning is right – and that's the only thing that makes you right.'

Warren Buffett, the world's most successful investor (value investing).

'I know from experience that nobody can give me a tip or a series of tips that will make more money for me than my own judgment.'

Edwin Lefevre (from his book *Reminiscences of a Stock Operator*). The comment is attributable to Jesse Livermore, the greatest stock market trader who ever lived.

'No matter what information you have, no matter what you are doing, you can be wrong.'
   Larry Hite, Mint Investment Management Company.

'You cannot teach a man anything; you can only help him to find it within himself.'
   Galileo Galilei.

'Investment, if you like, is a math exam where the powers that be work out the answers based on new formulae they develop after your papers have been handed in.'
   Dr Marc Faber, international stock market guru (famous bear).

'Money is a measurement of how well you're doing.'
   Robert Holmes à Court, international entrepreneur.

'Accurate thinkers permit no one to do their thinking for them.'
   Napoleon Hill, world-class motivational guru (from his book *Napoleon Hill's Unlimited Success*).

Fundamental analysis

'Countless incidents have demonstrated that a dollar of reported profits can easily prove to be worth less than 100 cents once the dust has settled.'
   Martin S Fridson, director, US investment bank Merrill Lynch (from his book *Investment Illusions*).

'Every set of published accounts is based on books which have been gently cooked or completely roasted.'
   Ian Griffiths (from his book *Creative Accounting*).

Opportunism

'Astronomic price earnings ratios rarely last for long, as they thrive on excessive hope and for that reason the most has to be made of them while they persist.'
   Jim Slater, private client guru (from the magazine *Analyst*).

High-tech stock investing

'I don't recommend Internet stocks to people who don't like massive risk, especially at current levels. People are jumping into it like it's a gold rush.'
    Bill Gates, founder of Microsoft (the world's richest man).

'If the share price divided by the annual research and development spend per share is five or less, then buy the shares of a technology company.'
    Conor McCarthy, founder, *TechInvest*, a high-tech stock tip sheet.

'To invest blindly in the TMT (technology, media and telecom) sector is a bit like assuming someone's bound to be good at cricket just because they're Australian.'
    Jonathan Maitland (from his book *How to Make Your Million from the Internet*).

Popular fallacies

'It is a myth that profits are higher in fast-growing industries.'
    John Kay, economist and academic.

'The children (or designated heirs) of a great CEO are about as likely to excel as replacement CEOs as are any of Beethoven's children to write great symphonies.'
    Robert A G Monks.

'Most investors don't even stop to consider how much business a company does. All they look at are earnings per share and net assets per share.'
    Kenneth L Fisher, stock market guru (from his classic book *Common Stocks and Uncommon Profits*).

'You do not need the expertise of a qualified accountant to achieve success.'
    Bernice Cohen, private client guru (from her book *The Armchair Investor*).

By the same author:

Everyone's Guide to Online Stock Market Investing

'Recommended reading for all active investors who prefer to make their own decisions. The pages are packed with understandable explanations and good financial advice.'
Terry Bond, private investor and Director of Proshare

'Davidson's useful and accessible book will help almost anyone develop their levels of expertise and knowledge of share market dynamics.'
Robert Cole, Editor of the 'Tempus' investment column in The Times

'No Internet hype, no unrealistic get-rich-quick claims – just proven advice for investors who want to make the most of online services. It really is a guide for everyone.'
Matthew Vincent, Head of Content, Investors Chronicle Online

How to Win in a Volatile Stock Market

'An excellent book.'
Business Daily

'The book. . . had all the promise of an interesting read. And this is just what it turned out to be. . . to get the most benefit, I would say read it sooner rather than later.'
Interactive Investor International (now Ample)

'Alexander Davidson's book could hardly have come at a better time. . . he has a strong opinion on everything and a lot of what he says is wonderfully provocative. . . The key quality – which in our view every investment book should possess – is that Davidson passionately believes in what he says. Not a single page is dull. . .'
Shares Magazine

Both the above titles are available from all good bookshops. To obtain further information, please contact the publisher at the address below:

Kogan Page Ltd
120 Pentonville Road
London N1 9JN
Tel: 020 7278 0433
Fax: 020 7837 6348
www.kogan-page.co.uk

Index

Page references in *italics* indicate figures.